John B Vaughter

Prison Life in Dixie

Third Edition

John B Vaughter

Prison Life in Dixie
Third Edition

ISBN/EAN: 9783744709057

Printed in Europe, USA, Canada, Australia, Japan

Cover: Foto ©ninafisch / pixelio.de

More available books at **www.hansebooks.com**

A STORM AT NIGHT—OUR MISERABLE QUARTERS.

PRISON LIFE

IN

DIXIE.

GIVING A SHORT HISTORY OF THE INHUMAN AND BARBAROUS TREATMENT OF OUR SOLDIERS BY REBEL AUTHORITIES.

BY

Rev. J. B. VAWTER.

(SERGEANT OATES.)

THIRD EDITION.

ILLUSTRATED WITH NUMEROUS FULL PAGE ENGRAVINGS.

TO WHICH IS ADDED THE SPEECH OF GEN. J. A. GARFIELD, DELIVERED AT THE ANDERSONVILLE REUNION, AT TOLEDO, OHIO, OCT. 3, 1879.

CHICAGO:
CENTRAL BOOK CONCERN.
1881.

DEDICATION.

TO THE SURVIVORS OF ANDERSONVILLE PRISON, MY COMRADES IN SUFFERING, THIS VOLUME IS DEDICATED.

PREFACE.

It is not claimed for this story that it gives a *full and perfect history* of the sufferings of the Union prisoners in the South during the war ; but the writer has endeavored to furnish such descriptions and incidents as will give the reader a true picture of Rebel Prisons, and the means and methods of living or dying in them.

In doing this, he has relied on his memory; selecting those facts, and trying to paint those pictures which are clearest and plainest in his own mind. He has not tried to color these descriptions —they would not bear it ; but has told them in plain language, just as they seem to him after a lapse of fifteen years.

ILLUSTRATIONS.

Storm at Night	1
Plan of Stockade	39
Result of Crossing the Dead-line	46
Distributing Rations	52
Breaking of the Stockade	64
Captured by Blood-hounds	107
Wanted a Shirt	114

CONTENTS.

CHAPTER I.

Sherman in front of Atlanta.—The Raid.—Sleepy Guards.—Pontoon Boats.—Rebel Camp Surrenders.—In the Enemy's Land.—Palmetto in Ashes.—A Running Fight.. 13

CHAPTER II.

A Southern Bridge.—Waiting for Stragglers.—Sharpshooters.—Bombshell.—The Capture................... 22

CHAPTER III.

Robbed.—Traded Hats.—A Rebel Woman.—Stored in a Cotton Warehouse.—Taken to Andersonville.—*Sumter Prison.*—The Stockade........................... 31

CHAPTER IV.

Arrival at Andersonville.—A Warning.—Hiding Valuables.—"Old Wirtz".—Stripped, Searched, Robbed and Turned in.—The Dead Line.—How We Obtained Thread... 40

CHAPTER V.

Our New Quarters.—"Nigger Peas."—Mode of Drawing Rations.—Always Hungry.—Vermin.—Horrible.—Fearful Mortality................................. 50

CHAPTER VI.

Cruelty of our Government.—Study of Human Nature.—Nothing to do.—Church Privileges.—A Catholic Priest.—August Storms.—A Water Spout.—Providence.—A Break in the Stockade.—A Dash for Liberty....... 59

CHAPTER VII.

Longing for News.—Nothing Reliable could be heard from the Rebels.—"Atlanta Gone to ——."—Moving Prisoners.—False Reports about Exchange.—Going out on a Dead Man's Name.—Crowded into Cars like Stock.—Wrecked................................. 68

CHAPTER VIII.

Taken Back to the Pen.—Plans of Escape.—Tunnels.—Bloodhounds.—Poor Drummer Boy.—Our Plan. .. 77

CHAPTER IX.

A Leap for Freedom.—Our Wardrobe.—A Friendly Alligator.—Traveling by Night...................... 85

CHAPTER X.

In the Swamps.—Discouraged.—A Fat Frog.—Flint River.—A Borrowed Canoe........................ 92

CHAPTER XI.

A Provoking Dilemma.—A Chance for Tyndall.—Swimming Rivers by Night.—Concealed in a Pile of Rags.—

A New Trouble.—Almost Starved.—Starve or Steal.—Hopes Growing Brighter.—A Familiar Sound.—Caught by Bloodhounds.—Rather Die than go back to Andersonville....... 98

CHAPTER XII.

Our Captors.—A Hospitality not before Encountered in the South.—Wanted, A Shirt.—The Situation Discussed.—Kindness.................................. 110

CHAPTER XIII.

On the Road.—A Mob.—Red-Tape Fops.—Jailed 119

CHAPTER XIV.

The Columbus Jail.—Better Fare.—To Macon.—New Plans for Escape.—Camp Lawton................ 126

CHAPTER XV.

False Promises of Exchange.—Searching for Acquaintances.—Presidential Election.—The Result........ 132

CHAPTER XVI.

Attempt to Entice Prisoners to make Shoes for the Rebel Army. The Temptation.—Enlistments.—Running the Gauntlet.—Another Change...................... 138

CHAPTER XVII.

Life on the Rail Road.—The Blues.—Great Excitement.—Sherman loose in Georgia.—Swamps.—A Country Residence.—"Poor White Trash."—A Citizen.......,... 143

CHAPTER XVIII.

"Flanking."—Exchange.—A Dash for Liberty.—Moved

Again.—A Square Meal.—Back to Andersonville... 150

CHAPTER XIX.

Andersonville in Winter.—The Weather.—How Fuel was Obtained.—Efforts to Keep Warm.—Good News.—Manufacturing Industries.—"Raising" Confed. Money.. 157

CHAPTER XX.

Sheds.—Spring has come.—Sighing for News.—Prospect for Exchange.—Left Alone.—Ready to die........ 165

CHAPTER XXI.

The Exchange Stopped.—Wilson's Raid.—New Hope.—Stocks.—A Hasty Move.—Another Plan to Escape.—Great Excitement Among the Rebs.—Rebel Lies.—Corralled for the Last Time......................... 173

CHAPTER XXII.

Preparations for Another Move.—Anxiously Waiting.—Rebel Advice.—Turned Loose.—A Pathetic Scene.—Tears and Curses.—Manifestations of Joy at Sight of the Old Flag.—God's Country.................... 183

CHAPTER XXIII.

Homeward Bound.—A Feast.—Too Happy to Sleep.—On the Atlantic.—Ice for the Sick(?).—Home at Last. 192

Speech of Gen. Garfield at the Andersonville Reunion, at Toledo, Ohio, Oct. 5, 1879....................... 199

Andersonville in 1880............................. 206

CHAPTER I.

THE RAID.

While Sherman's army lay in front of Atlanta, he determined to send his cavalry on a raid to the enemy's rear, to destroy their railroad communication. So, on July 27th, 1864, General Stoneman moved eastward to pass around the flank of the rebel army, and General Ed. McCook, at the same time, started to pass around the left.

McCook's command numbered about 2,000 men, well mounted and equipped, of which the writer was one.

We all knew the nature of the mission on which we were sent, and felt that it was difficult. For it is not easy for two thousand men to go behind a hostile army of sixty thousand, and do any damage, and—get back.

Early on that bright, hot July morning, the bugle called us into line—an inspection was made, and all lame horses or sick men ordered back to camp. We consoled those who had to stay behind with the promise that we would bring them a plug of tobacco when we came back. *When we came back?* We shall see.

Thus relieved of all that would encumber us, we moved out on the road and started westward. We crossed the Chattahoochee at Sandtown, and passed down on the west side about twenty miles to the vicinity of Campbelltown, when the command was ordered to rest under cover of the woods, and scouts sent out to find a place at which to cross the river. The different scouting parties returned with reports that all the fords and ferries were fortified and guarded by rebel infantry.

About midnight we again mounted, and under cover of the darkness, with no sound but the tread of our horses on the sandy road, we crept down the river about five miles farther, to an old, deserted ferry. Two companies were stationed at this point, and they had a picket-post on our side of the river; four men and an officer were on guard, but thinking the Yanks were far away they had set their guns against a tree, built a little fire to smoke off the mosquitoes, and were quietly snoozing when our scouts crept up, moved the guns from the tree, and then, with their own guns cocked and ready, waked up the pickets and told them to keep very quiet, as we wished to cross the river without disturbing any one.

We halted on the river bank, our pontoon wagons were ordered up, and we had two boats made and launched in a few minutes.

For many of our readers, I will state that the pontoons taken by the cavalry on their raids were light frames that could be put together or taken apart in a moment. When the frame or skeleton was put together, a cloth of thick canvas was stretched over it, fastened at the corners, and it was ready to launch. The material for a boat twenty feet long, six wide, and two deep, could be carried in a very small space.

Four companies crossed, and deployed along the east bank; the rest drew up in line on the west shore and waited for day. As soon as it was light enough, the troops on the east side surrounded the rebel camp, and they surrendered without firing a gun.

Preparations were at once begun for crossing the river, but it was almost noon before the entire command was across.

From here the pontoon wagons were sent back under a guard. Our prisoners were turned loose because we had no way of taking care of them, and we started rapidly across the country in search of the Atlanta & West Point railroad.

When we left the river, after seeing our bridge taken out on the other side, we recognized that we were no longer a part of the great army before Atlanta, but a detached brigade in the enemy's land, with a powerful army between us and our campground. The news of the raid would spread like a prairie fire; we would be headed off, followed up, and harrassed. Our safety lay in rapid movement.

We traveled well that afternoon. At about eight o'clock, in the midst of a thunder shower, we came upon the railroad near the town of Palmetto.

We deployed a skirmish line and moved on the town. A company of rebel cavalry fired one volley and fled, and we posted a heavy picket to prevent surprise, and went to work. The rain ceased by the time we were fairly at work, and the stars came out.

We tore down the telegraph wire, wound up a quarter of a mile of it, and sunk it in a pond. We tore up as much railroad track, made fires of the ties, and piled the rails on them, so as to heat and bend them.

There were a half-dozen freight cars on the side track, and a large quantity of bacon in the depot, and four or five warehouses filled with baled cotton near the track. These were fired—and what a terrible fire they made! The whole town and surrounding country were lit up by the red glare.

The clouds overhead reflected the light and shone like red sunset. The fire became so hot that no one could pass along the street. It spread to adjacent buildings. The citizens were seen scampering in all directions. Even women—some of them in their night clothes, with white, scared faces—flitted from alley to street and from street to alley. Palmetto at sunset knew that there was war in the land, but she lay down secure in the feeling that she had a grand army in front of her to defend her from invasion. Before midnight she realized that war—destructive, terrible, cruel—was in her midst. The next morning arose upon a blackened ruin. It was the track of war.

A little before midnight our work was done, and we swept out of town toward the east. Just east of town we passed a plantation where two or three hundred negroes, of all ages and sexes, were sitting on the fence watching the red glare of the burning village. The light was bright enough to make everything distinct. As we rode by, one old "aunty" raised her hands toward heaven and cried aloud, "Bress de Lord! de jubilee hab come!"

At about three o'clock A. M., we came upon a large park of army wagons; we were told that there were eight hundred of them. Hood had sent them back there to have them safe. We took the mules, burned the wagons, and turned the drivers loose.

At about seven o'clock that morning we struck the Macon railroad near Lovejoy station, where we expected to form a junction with Stoneman, who had started around the other way.

We treated this road like we did the other; captured and destroyed a train of cars, and sent out scouts in all directions to feel for Stoneman.

Some of our scouts came back to tell us that there was rebel cavalry near us. Some did not come back at all. No word or sign from Stoneman could we get. We feared he was in trouble, or "gone up," but we wanted some word.

But as evidence multiplied that the Johnnies were thickening around us, we all became impatient. Croxton and Brownlow were chafing like caged tigers. They felt that waiting was fatal. (I have always believed that Croxton could have taken us out of the scrape.) But McCook was loth to leave without first learning the fate of Stoneman.

About two o'clock P. M. he gave it up. By this time the rebs had surrounded us, and were just waiting to see how we would try to get out. We skirmished with them for an hour, feeling their line on the west and south, and losing five or six men killed. We then massed our forces, and charging up a ravine, broke their line and fled; and all that afternoon, and the night following, we had a running fight, they crowding our rear the whole time.

Whenever they would get too close, one or two companies of our command would be deployed to skirmish with them. This would cause them to halt and form for attack, and thus give us a little time. True, these companies were often captured, but they were sacrificed to save the rest of the command.

CHAPTER II.

THE CAPTURE.

The first chapter closed with our flight after we cut through the rebel's line near Lovejoy station. Twice during the afternoon they pressed our rear so closely that we were obliged to deploy a skirmish line and show fight, in order to gain time. But after dark, we rode on without hearing or seeing anything of our pursuers, and the hope that they had encamped for the night was struggling for a place in our minds; though, really, our knowledge of our pursuers (Wheeler's cavalry) gave us small room for hope.

The night was warm; there was no wind, and a haze crept up, till the only stars visible were those near the zenith.

About midnight we came to a little river. We approached it, coming down a sloping hillside for perhaps two hundred yards, through a scrubby growth of oak, known as oak barrens, which is common in many parts of the South. The road had been changed about on this hillside till there were five or six parallel tracks and ditches running among the brush.

A bridge of Southern style spanned this river. Let me describe it: Three cribs, or pens of logs, 6x16 feet, and ten feet high, are placed about twenty feet apart in the river. These are connected with each other and with the shore by four round "sleepers" to each span. The bridge is then floored with split slabs, or puncheons. The banks of the river were about as high as the cribs.

After crossing this bridge the road runs across a bottom of about fifty or sixty yards, and then turns an oblique angle to the right, and keeps along the foot of the hill for awhile. A field fills up the bottom land between the road and the river, reaching down to the bridge.

When we came to this bridge, my company (C) was ordered to remain behind and guard it for half an hour, in order to let our stragglers get across, and then to burn it.

These stragglers were men whose horses had failed in the run of the three days and nights since we started, till they couldn't keep up.

Our company flanked out, and as soon as the rest of the command filed past, we dismounted. Number fours took our horses up around the turn in the road, about a quarter of a mile, and held them.

This left us forty-six men to guard and burn the bridge. Tom B—— was detailed to go to the top of the hill in the barrens, and stand picket. The rest of us pulled down ten or fifteen panels of rail-fence, and carried the rails onto the bridge for kindling, and built up a good fire on the ground to have plenty of brands to stick into it when the word should be given.

The memory of that night forms a clear, distinct picture. As our fire burned in the road, lighting up the bridge and shining against the trees, and throwing dark shadows on the muddy waters in the river, forty-five men stood and looked each other in the face. Not a solitary straggler had come to the bridge since we stopped. What did it mean? To the old soldier it meant that the sleepless foe was near. It might be a good time to think of home and friends, or we might—

"Who goes there?"

"Who the — are you?"

Bang! Bang!

It was Tom's challenge, and the answer left no doubt as to who was challenged. One bullet went singing to the north, the other buried itself in the bridge at our feet. Tom came down the hill double-quick. He did not know whether he hit his man or not.

We stuck our fire among the rails and retreated to the bend in the road. Just around the turn the road was washed out into a kind of ditch, and by lying down in it, we had a full sweep of the bridge through the bottom crack of the rail-fence. Here we halted to watch our fire till it would get beyond the possibility of being put out.

For a few minutes all was still. Our fire was beginning to take hold of the bridge, and we were thinking of running for our horses, when suddenly a sheet of flame flashed out of the brush for a quarter of a mile up the river, followed by a tremendous crash.

They had crept up and formed in silence, and were pouring a deadly fire into the thicket that lined the south bank. After a few rounds and no reply, we heard the command:

"Onto the bridge and throw off that fire. Quick!"

About a hundred men came out of the brush and crowded onto the bridge.

We lay in that ditch, and thrust the muzzles of our guns through the lowest crack in the fence. They were in a strong light. We waited until the bridge was full, and the foremost man had reached the fire and began to throw off the rails. Then we let them have it. The range was about seventy-five yards. Some fell on the bridge, some went over its sides into the river, and some retreated. We cleared the bridge; nobody could stand our well-directed fire. We drew their fire toward us. A shower of balls battered against the fence, and as many passed over us, but we were not hit. We never attempted to answer their fire; but whenever a man showed himself about the bridge, we plugged him.

The fire got under good headway, and we slipped up that ditch and ran to our horses, mounted, and made our best speed to overtake our command. We caught up just as morning began to dawn. As soon as it was light we halted to feed; but before our horses were half done eating, the rebels were upon us again. Knowing the country better than we did, they had crossed the river at another place, and dashed on to cut us off from Chattahoochee.

We tried to make a stand, but they outnumbered us, and flanked us, and we were forced to save ourselves by flight.

We came into the neighborhood of Newman, and found that eight thousand infantry were there prepared to receive us. With these fresh troops before us and Wheeler's cavalry behind us, we found ourselves in a fix. But worn out as we and our horses were, we charged, and fought our way to the right, and would have reached the Chattahoochee if we could have found a road.

By this time we were demoralized. We had all lost confidence in McCook. I don't believe there was a man in the brigade that would have paid any attention to him after we passed Newman. But curses, bitter and deep, were heaped on him on all sides.

We broke up into squads, following our own regimental or company commanders, or, still worse, two or three old comrades swearing to live or die together, and going on their own hook.

A good many of us stuck to Lieut.-Col. Kelley, and rode through the woods till we got into a piece of swampy ground near the river, where our horses mired. We dismounted. There I parted from Bombshell; a better mare never grew upon Kentucky bluegrass. We had fared together for a thousand miles, had drank and bathed in a hundred rivers. She had never known any other master, and I was more partner than master. I hope she died in that swamp, and that no Johnnie ever had her to show as a trophy of that chase, or rode her against that flag she had followed so long. Alas! poor Bombshell! She did not fully understand all the questions involved in the war, but she was a true soldier.

Leaving our horses, we tried to get to the river on foot, intending to swim it and escape, if possible. But as we came out of the jungle, we fronted a battalion of cavalry. Their guns were aimed.

"Halt!"

We threw up our hands, and they rode down on us to receive our arms.

We had in Company A of our regiment a man who deserted the rebels at the battle of Perryville, and enlisted with us. As the rebs came down, he recognized his old comrades, and knowing he would be shot anyway, he resolved to sell his life for all it would bring. So, as they came up, he shot the Major through the heart, killing him at once. The next instant he fell among us riddled with balls, and his rash deed came near causing the death of every one of us.

"Kill every —— —— —— ——!" cried a rebel officer in excitement.

Just then we saw Wheeler and staff, and called to him. The Johnnies pointed to their dead officer and claimed treachery. But the General ordered them to guard us as prisoners, and not to shoot any one who surrendered.

They took charge of us.

"Give me that gun." I handed it up. "Give me your cartridge-box." "Here it is." "Give me that poncho—give me that blanket."

I think the troop that captured us was a battalion of the Third Texas Cavalry.

CHAPTER III.

TAKEN TO ANDERSONVILLE.

There were fifty or sixty of us together when captured in the edge of the swamp. After disarming us we were taken a short distance to a road. Here we were halted and guarded, while the rebs scoured the woods and continued the pursuit. The report of firearms was heard far and near, and every little while a squad of prisoners would be added to our company, till we numbered over three hundred, when they started us toward Newman.

By talking together we learned much of the extent of our disaster. We learned from some of Brownlow's men that he had crossed the Chattahoochee, swimming his horse; a few of his men got across with him, a number were shot in the river, and those who told me the story were captured on the east bank. This Col. Brownlow was a son of the famous old Parson of East Tennessee. He had a good deal of the Old Parson in him, and owing to certain deeds performed in former raids in his own country, he knew it was best for him to keep out of rebel hands. I was glad to learn afterwards that he succeeded in reaching our lines, much to their disappointment.

. The troops who were guarding us were Texans, and did not scruple to rob us of any private property that caught their eye. Our ponchos were in demand. Then they robbed most of us of our canteens. Of course we gave them up under protest. None but an old soldier can appreciate our loss in these. We also swapped hats and boots with them, utterly destroying our faith in the old maxim that "it takes two to make a bargain."

My boots were too small for any that tried them, and I was allowed to keep them; but my neat, soft felt hat of the Burnside pattern, was lifted off my head by a long-haired fellow, who gave me in exchange his C. S. regulation tile. Every old soldier remembers the old white hats that we found scattered over every battle-field and camp ground out of which we chased the Johnnies, from the Ohio River to the Gulf of Mexico.

To the reader who was not in the army I will say, the hat that I received was made of white wool, felted about a quarter of an inch thick, and when I got it it was a light gray color, and was about the size and shape of an old washpan. I wore it to prison, and for many long months it served me for a shelter from the hot sun, for a cushion to sit on when the sand was too hot to be comfortable, and for a pillow at night. After sitting around in the rain all day, I think it would have weighed five pounds.

When they got ready to start toward Newman, we were marched along the road in four ranks, with Rebels to right of us, Rebels to left of us, Rebels in front of us— it spoils the poetry—Rebels behind us.

They rode. We walked. It was hot and dusty. Remember we had been in the saddle both the preceding nights, and were tired and sleepy.

As we passed a house one of the rebel officers called at the gate for a drink of water. A nice-looking lady came out, accompanied by a black girl who bore the pitcher. She gave him and two or three others a drink, and they gave her a boastful account of how they had scooped us. She then turned toward us and our guard, and with a pleasant smile asked, "Would any of you soldiers like a drink?" One of our boys said, "Madam, I would like a drink, please." The smile faded out and a look of contempt took its place, as she answered, "*You low-flung, thieving Yank— would I give* you *a drink?* Not unless it had strychnine in it. You *ought to be hung,* every one of you!"

I write this incident because it helps to

show the feeling of the South toward the Union army.

We got to Newman about the middle of the afternoon, and were put in an old cotton warehouse and closely guarded. When we entered that warehouse we found four or five hundred of our comrades already in. Our greetings were not joyous, the usual form being, "*What? You, too!* I was in hopes you had escaped."

They kept adding to our numbers till night, and by that time a majority of the command that left Sherman's lines four days before was in the hands of the enemy. And what added to the bitterness of our capture was that we felt that it was due to the incompetence of our leader.

They kept us at Newman that night and the next day while they mended the railroad at Palmetto. As soon as they could get a train through they moved us to East Point, a junction only six miles from Atlanta. Here we lay one night and day, in hearing of Sherman's guns. From there we were taken to Andersonville, arriving there about noon, August 2d.

Andersonville is a small town on the Macon & S. W. R. R. At that time it did not contain over a dozen houses, and most of these were poor shanties. There were only two or three respectable residences. There was one store, kept in part of the depot building, and a cotton warehouse. The cotton warehouse is to a Georgia railroad station what the grain elevator is in Iowa. The town was built in a pine forest, many of the stumps and a few of the trees still remaining in the streets and yards, and the woods encroaching on it at almost every point.

A little brook ran through the town, furnishing a natural sewer for its filth and offal. Just east of the village was the rebel camp of three or four thousand troops, mostly Georgia militia, composed of men too old and boys too young for field service. These were the prison guard.

Still farther to the east, about half a mile from the station, was the pen, called by the rebs "*Sumter prison*," but known all over the North as Andersonville Prison Pen. This pen was about fifty rods long and thirty-six wide. It lay across the same brook that ran through the village and the rebel camp. The stream ran to the east. It divided the pen into two parts, known to us as "North side" and "South side." North side contained about seven and a half acres, South side about three and a half.

The prison wall was of hewn timber, placed on end six feet in the ground, and extending twelve feet above ground—making a solid wall eight inches thick. Near the top of this wall, on the outside, were platforms, or sentry-boxes, with sheds built over them to keep off the sun and rain, so that the guard had a comfortable place in which to stand and watch what was going on in the pen. There were about fifty of these boxes around the stockade.

There were two gates, a "north" and a "south" gate, both on the west side of the pen. Here again north and south have reference to sides of the brook. These gates were small stockade pens, about thirty feet square, with heavy doors, opening into the prison on one side and outside on the other. If the inner door was opened the outer door was always shut, and vice versa.

There was another wall outside the one I have named, about two hundred feet from it, running part way round. This outer wall was not continuous, but had large openings in it, in which artillery was placed in such position that they could rake the prison with grape or shell if they so desired.

From the north side, by looking over the stockade where it crossed the hollow, we could see Wirtz's headquarters above, and our hospital below. From the south side, in looking over the same way, we could see the quarters of a pack of blood hounds, "the old Redfield," and a part of the town.

EXPLANATION OF STOCKADE.
(See next page.)

1. STOCKADE.
2. "DEAD LINE."
3. BROOK.
4. SWAMP.
5. REBEL SUTTLERS.
6. BAKE-HOUSE FOR CORN-BREAD.
8 & 9. ENTRANCES.
10 & 11. OUTER STOCKADES.
12. EARTHWORK FORTIFICATIONS.
13. LOCATION OF HOSPITAL.
14. PLACE WHERE THE SURGEONS PRESCRIBED FOR THE SICK AND ADMITTED TO THE HOSPITAL.

PRISON LIFE IN DIXIE. 39

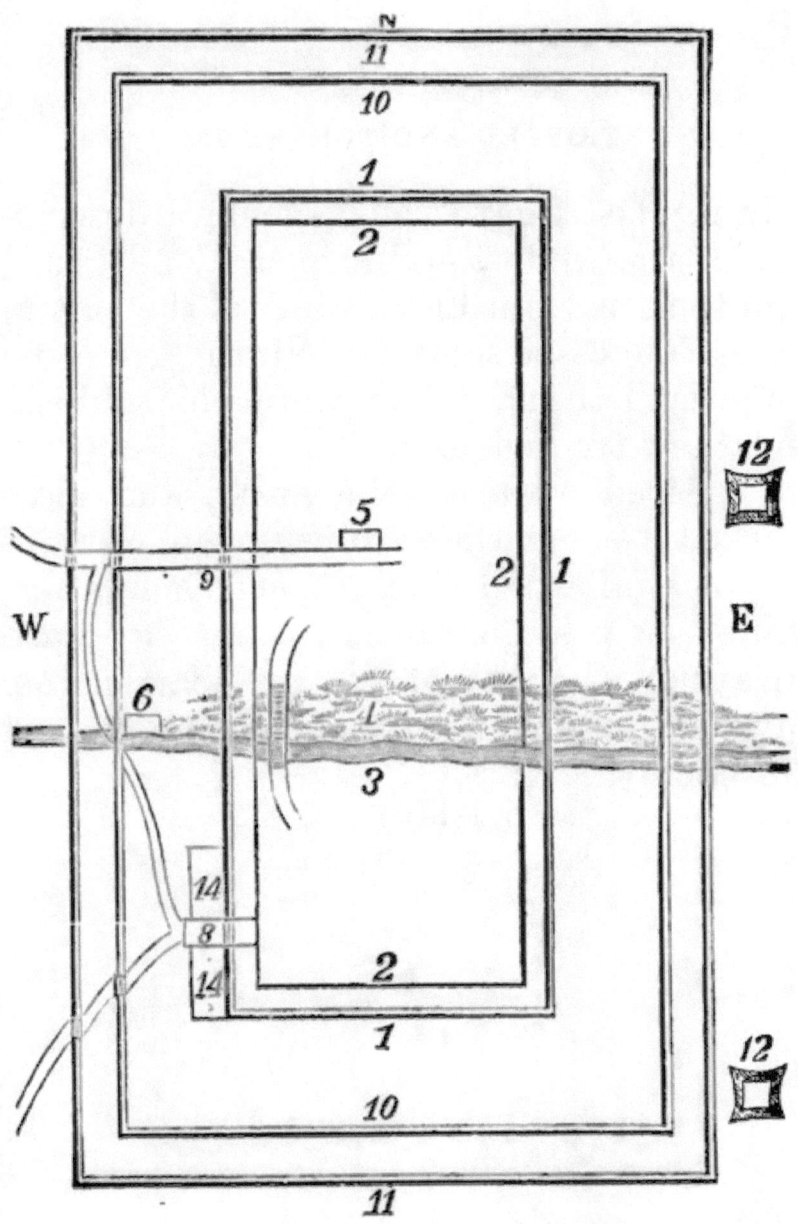

PLAN OF STOCKADE. 13.

CHAPTER IV.

STRIPPED AND TURNED IN.

In my last I gave you a general description of the Andersonville pen. The guard who took us from East Point to the prison were Tennessee soldiers—Ninth Tennessee Infantry, I think. They were old soldiers, and they treated us well.

I noticed while in the army, and have marked it since, that soldiers who were *in the front,* on either side, respect each other; while the post guards and others who are always in the rear of the real battle line, have a great contempt for the prowess of the enemy.

When our train came to a stop at the Andersonville depot, we saw about twenty men, dressed in what had once passed for Confederate uniforms, but so ragged and dirty as to be past recognition. They were loading wagons, and occasionally one of them passed close to the train. They never looked at us, but as they passed close by they were repeating over and over, as though they would forget it, this song: "If you have any money, hide it. If you have any valuables, hide them."

We took it as a sign and acted on it. Some ripped a small hole and slipped money in the hems and collars of blouses, some in boots—every safe place you could think of. I had one ten-dollar bill. I folded it small, peeled off the outside leaf of a plug of "Ole Verginny," wrapped it carefully around my bill, and laid it in my cheek. I didn't chew that quid very vigorously.

As the rebs had to detail a guard of militia after we got there, we had ample time for all this hiding, and our Tennessee guards paid no attention to our efforts.

About two o'clock the guard came and took us off the cars. They marched us through the rebel camp, and about half way between it and the pen, on a sloping plain of bright yellow sand, they halted us and opened us into single ranks. After waiting awhile here, the sun roasting our heads and the sand stewing our feet, old Wirtz came out with a squad of men to search us. This was my first view of that notorious Switzer. He was dressed in a suit of white duck, with a Panama hat, and riding a white horse.

He rode down our lines and cursed us for being raiders; then gave his commands so that all could hear:

"If any man stoops down, or sits down, or tries to hide any thing, shoot him!"

"Strip 'im! Take eberyting he got! I I make 'im tink it is hell!"

I would not write this last sentence if I thought there was anything profane about it; but after a few month's suffering in that horrid pen, I concluded the old Dutchman had not even used the hyperbole, but had simply stated a fact in strong language.

Two large boxes were brought to put the plunder in, and the search was begun. They made us take off all our clothes and lay them out in front of us, and stand there naked while they searched them. They turned all the pockets, then felt all the seams and hems, and if they felt a lump, they would throw that garment on their pile. They took and kept all watches, rings, knives, money, pipes, and even pictures of wives and sweethearts. One boy tried to make out that he could not get his ring off.

"If te ring no come off, *take te finger,*" said Wirtz.

After they were satisfied with their examination, they would throw back such garments as they allowed us to have. If we had any extras about our clothes they kept them. I went through and retained shirt, blouse and pants. My blouse and pants were pretty good, my shirt was well worn. They kept my boots, but allowed me the hat I received of the Texan.

I learned afterwards that they did not always strip prisoners quite so closely as they did us. A whole brigade, captured at Plymouth, N. C., and called by the other prisoners, "Plymouth pilgrims," came into the pen with their blankets and overcoats. Their good luck was exceptional. The Western troops were stripped worse than the Eastern, and cavalry worse than infantry. Their excuse for this was that the Western cavalry was always raiding and destroying their property.

After being searched, we were taken to the north gate; a door was opened in the gate-pen (a kind of ante-room, thirty feet square), and ninety men were crowded into it. The door was then closed, and another door was opened into the prison, and we were counted again as we passed through. Then a new ninety were let in and counted through, and so on to the end. I never knew why they kept us in nineties, but they did. Each ninety was counted every day, and we drew rations from that count.

Thus we entered Andersonville prison. Remember it was about thirty-six by fifty rods, containing about eleven acres, with a wall twelve feet high around it, and a little brook running through it.

About twenty feet from the wall, ran a row of stakes with a slender rail tacked on them; this was the "dead line." In some places the rail had been knocked off, and only the stakes marked the boundary between life and death; for if any one crossed the line, he was shot without warning.

This leads me to make a remark on the "dead-lines," which were common to all Southern prisons. Sometimes this line was, as at Andersonville, within a stockade, and the guard were stationed upon the wall upon the alert to pick off any unfortunate who was so incautious as to step over. In some cases the prisons were temporary, and had not even a stockade. A rope was drawn; and if any prisoner, for the sake of wood, water, or any other cause, stepped beyond it, an instantaneous shot warned all others to beware of his untimely fate.

When our command got in, there were *thirty-three thousand men in that pen!* Can you realize that fact? Take the entire population of two average counties in Iowa

THE RESULT OF CROSSING THE DEAD LINE.

or Illinois, and crowd them onto eleven acres, and you have not enough then. Reduce it, and you find that you have about eighteen men to the square rod. Some of these men had a little shelter of their own providing. Some took two sticks about four feet long, stuck them in the ground about six feet apart, fixed a little pole from one to the other, fastened one edge of a blanket to the pole, and, drawing the other edge back till it was straight, piled sand enough on it to hold it, or took wooden pins and pinned it to the ground.

Such a tent, or shade, answered for four men. I have known six to occupy one. Of course they could not all lie down under it, but they could all squat under it to keep off the sunshine. If a party had no blanket, they could sometimes make a substitute by ripping up pants, shirts, jackets, etc., and sewing them together. These garments were obtained by stripping the dead.

If a man had money, he could buy sacks (made of strong, coarse cotton cloth) of the quartermaster who issued our rations. At the time of our capture, sacks two feet wide and three feet long cost two dollars each in greenbacks, or eight in confed. Thread to sew with was obtained by raveling out a piece of sack. Sometimes we drew rations in these sacks, and could keep them until ration time the next day. When this was the case, we were bound to return the sack or lose our next ration; but we could cut off the bottom of it two or three inches and not be detected, if we sewed it up as it had been. These strips furnished thread for the ninety.

About two hundred prisoners were detailed outside, on parole, to help handle rations, to cook, and to dig trenches to bury in, etc. It was they who warned us to hide our money at the depot. They slept in the gate, or ante-room, of nights—at least part of them did. Through them we obtained the stakes and poles to put up our meager tents. When the inside door would be opened of a morning, they would pitch them in beyond the dead-line to their friends. If you had no friend out on parole, the set, two stakes four feet long, and a pole six feet long, would cost you fifty cents.

The "Plymouth pilgrims" nearly all had blanket tents, such as I have described, and a good many others had something that would at least partly keep the sun off; but the majority of that vast crowd had no shelter of any kind. They entered there *stripped and robbed.* The dew beaded their hair and beard at night, and they sweltered under that burning sun, and groveled in that roasting sand by day. *What had they done? Answered their country's call, and followed its flag.*

CHAPTER V.

HORRIBLE.

All the space was claimed and occupied before we got there. Just imagine one or two of those half-faced tents on every square rod, and ten or twelve men without shelter claiming room on the same.

Some one claimed every foot. The first few nights we just dropped down wherever we could find room enough, and refused to move for threats, curses, or lice, and we certainly had full rations of each.

Four of us determined to stick together, and after hunting two or three days we found a place six feet square, about the middle of the south side. Five men had owned it, but three were dead, and the other two were willing to vacate for a small consideration. We bought three sacks and made us a shelter. It took a week to get used to the horrid place.

During this crowded period we drew cooked rations. Our bread was made of unsifted meal and water, without salt, or anything to lighten it; baked in large sheets about two inches thick. When cut up into single rations, each man received a piece about two by three inches, and as thick as the sheet or loaf. In addition to this, we received about half a pint of cooked beans or peas. They were raised in the South to feed slaves, and were called the "nigger peas," but I think they are really a species of coarse black bean. There is one thing in favor of the "Pea" theory, however. They were almost invariably full of bugs, and as issued to us, the bugs were the only seasoning they had. Once in a while a small ration of rice was given in place of the beans. About twice a week we received a small ration of meat. If pork, about one

DISTRIBUTING RATIONS.

ounce per man; if beef, about two ounces. Sometimes in place of the meat, we drew about two spoonfuls of molasses per man.

We drew our rations from two to three o'clock P. M. Whatever we got we ate at once, and then fasted until that hour the next day. We were hungry all the time,—even just after we had eaten. This hunger colored our conversation. Drop into a group of talkers, and you would hear some one describing a feast he had enjoyed; or drawing on his imagination for one he intended to order, if he ever got out alive. One poor boy who lay near us would wind up every such talk with: "Fried pork, sausage, and pancakes is good enough for me." Even in our sleep we were not free; but our rest was full of dreams of loaded tables, with always something to prevent us from partaking of their viands, till we would wake up. Like the old toper who dreamed he had a pint of whisky, and thought to make a hot punch, but while his water was heating he woke up. He turned over, smacked his lips, and remarked: "What a fool I was not to drink that cold!"

At least two-thirds of the men were sick. Half of them had diarrhea, and our coarse rations aggravated the disease. Among the older prisoners scurvy was common. About five thousand men were past helping themselves. They were lying all over the pen, many of them half naked, under a burning sun, and stinking in their filth. They could not help it, poor boys; and we could do nothing for them. We had no means. The whole camp literally swarmed with vermin. The sand was full of fleas, all alive with them. Lice crawled every-where. Flies swarmed in myriads. Blow-flies were upon the helpless, the dying and the dead. When the sun went down mosquitoes came in clouds from the swamps below. One mercy amid this woe, was that, soon after a man became too weak to help himself he generally became unconscious.

As soon as a man was dead he was carried to the south gate. At first they had a shed made of brush outside of the stockade, and the dead were carried out there. But one day an old scurvy skeleton *played* dead, and was carried out and laid with the rest.

He watched his chance and tried to crawl off and escape, but was caught and brought back. After that there was no more carrying outside, but we piled them up by the dead-line at the south gate.

We had a rule that whoever carried out a corpse should have what was on it. That looks bad, but it was all the chance to keep the living from going naked. The average mortality during August was one hundred and thirty per day.

Every forenoon lay at the south gate that hundred and thirty naked, haggard, and horribly discolored bodies, putrifying in the sun. It was a sight to sicken the stoutest. About ten or eleven o'clock they would come in with a wagon and pile those corpses into it, like cord-wood, and haul them to the old red field, where they were laid side by side in a long trench. After noon that same wagon would bring in our rations.

The little brook flowed with a gentle current three or four feet wide and four inches deep. Just below the dead-line, where it entered, we had a place scraped out eight feet wide, by twenty long, and nearly two deep. We kept that pool as clean as we could, to drink from. It was not clean even then, as the filth of the town and rebel camp washed into it from above. Below this were a number of circular pools ten or twelve feet in diameter, and two feet deep in the center, to wash in. There was always a crowd about these pools, from early morning till late at night, and yet I believe half the men in that pen never washed at all. So many were discouraged by their afflictions, and losing all hope, lost decency and self-respect with it, and laid down in their filth and died.

Near the brook, on each side, were a good many holes, or shallow wells, dug down to its level. The water in these, being filtered through the sand, was thought to be purer than the brook water, though none of it was good.

Below the wash pools, which did not extend half way down, this little brook became the privy sink for the whole camp. I have studied for a week how I might write a description of our sufferings and leave this out; but my chapter of horrors would not be complete without it. Thirty thousand men, most of them sick, had to use about one hundred yards of this branch. Gradually the filth clogged up the opening in the stockade, making a dam. As filth accumulated it rose and spread out over the banks, until it became three or four feet deep—spread forty feet wide, and backed up the stream seventy-five yards—making in our midst a lake, the horror of which made other troubles seem light by comparison. It was worked over and over by masses of great slimy maggots an inch long. The sun pouring his heat into it all day generating poisonous gases. At night the damp air was loaded with a stench that cried to heaven for vengeance. It became so poisonous that if any one having a sore, if only a mosquito bite, should by accident step into the nasty mass, it would cause gangrene.

I have seen men, weak and sick, stagger down to that place during the hot part of the day. The foul odors and the heat would overcome them, and they would faint and fall into the reeking mass. Some one would drag them out onto the dry ground, and they would lie there and die in the filth, those great slimy maggots crawling over them, even in their nostrils and mouths before they were dead. I saw five men die thus in one day.

If I *alone* knew these things I would be afraid to tell them. They would be hard to believe. But the survivors of that prison are scattered all over the North. Many of them are men of known character. Ask any of them if I have exaggerated or even colored this description. They will tell you, No'

CHAPTER VI.

PROVIDENCE.

"How did you spend your time?"

For a while we could hold interesting chats. But we soon wore out all the interesting incidents of our lives, exhausted our supply of anecdotes and stories; and were left with nothing to talk of, except to describe different dishes of food that we wanted, or to curse the rebels for their treatment, and to grumble at our Government for not exchanging us. These were standard themes; they could be repeated, in the same words, every day in the month, and every hour in the day, and always be interesting.

Among all those crowds a good laugh was seldom heard. Our gayest, jolliest soldiers soon became gloomy and silent; and wit and humor took on the morbid form of saying grotesque and horrid things about our misfortunes.

The study of human nature there would fill with sadness any who love the race. The best elements seemed to die, and the worst held high carnival in our souls. Men were brutal, selfish, cross and mean to each other. The strongest struggled for life, and the weak died without pity. A dying man might ask a dozen for a drink before he would find one to bring it to him, unless he had comrades who had known him before he got into the pen. Of course there were a few exceptions. Too few. Yet these men were not Modocs, nor Australian bushmen. Some of them belonged to the rough classes, but many were refined, cultivated gentlemen, the light of the social circle, the pride of an enlightened home. But they were treated by their foes worse than brutes

Their own Government refused to exchange, and abandoned them, and they became desperate.

Time dragged heavily. Nothing to do; nothing to read. Some whiled away the hours playing chess. "Where did you get chessboards and men?" We marked out a place on the ground for a board, and made our set of men by notching sticks so that we would know them. When we moved a piece, we stuck it in the ground so it would stand. I learned this fascinating game with such a set. Though there were a few who had *boards* of their own making.

There were church privileges for those who wanted them. That is, there were four or five places where these ragged, scurvied, filthy, vermin-eaten wretches met twice a week and tried to worship God. They were generally informal social meetings. They sang old-fashioned hymns, like "O thou fount," or "Rock of Ages,"—hymns that are as much a part of our civilization as the steam engine is. They squatted on the ground, and slapped mosquitoes, and scratched, while one of their number read a portion of the Scripture, led in prayer, or gave an exhortation.

About ten or fifteen took active part, but they usually had a large audience of respectful listeners. At one place, on the south side, near my quarters, I think the average audience would number one thousand. I used to frequently attend as a listener. There was no attempt to preach any doctrine except faith in God. The Scripture lessons were usually from Psalms, and some of David's prayers for his enemies sounded so much like cursing the rebels that even the carnal-minded could say "Amen."

While writing of the religious exercises, I will not omit the ministry of a Catholic priest. He visited the prison regularly, giving the consolations of his church to the sick, shriving the dying, and sprinkling holy water on the dead. He was willing to talk to any one who cared for religious conversation. He seemed very industrious and earnest in his work.

Suppose that of the thirteen thousand buried in that old field, there will be *one* who will at last arise justified through

Christ. And suppose that the judgment shall be as Jesus described it. If so, of all the ministers in Georgia, accessible to Andersonville, *only one* could hear this sentence, "I was sick and in prison and ye visited me," and that one is a Catholic.

Protestant churches may warn us of the danger of the Papal power, but till some of us learn *this lesson* of visiting the prisons, the hospitals, the plague-stricken and the outcast, we will never lead the masses away from Catholicism.

During August we had several thunder showers. But there is one that in Andersonville history will always stand alone as eminently "the storm."

About the last of the month (I had no way to keep dates and can't remember them exactly), it came up suddenly, about midday, accompanied by vivid lightning and loud thunder, and a rain-fall such as is called the bursting of a water-spout. With the first dash, we were drenched. In a few minutes the ground was covered with water, and great streams were rushing down the hillsides, washing deep gullies

BREAKING OF THE STOCKADE.

through our beds, and in other places almost burying the helpless in sand and water. And still it rained. The lightning seemed to dance over the ground, and the thunder roared like a park of artillery. The brook began to raise, and was soon too large to get through the vents made for it in the stockade. It dammed up at both walls till it almost reached the top. The upper wall gave way, and a flood eight or ten feet deep and fifty wide was rushing through the pen. When it struck the lower wall, it, too, fell with a crash. A hundred brave men rushed into the boiling flood to ride out on it. A shell from the battery fizzed over our heads. The long roll sounded, and the whole guard rushed to the openings, and stood in the rain along that rushing stream with fixed bayonets, to keep us in. The storm finally spent itself. Clouds rolled away. The sun came out. The angry waters subsided. The rebs went to work to repair the walls.

"What of it?" That reeking, pestilential lake of filth, that I described in the last chapter, was gone. A sand-bar three or four feet deep was formed where part of it had been. The stream had formed a new channel for itself, and the rest of it was washed out to the very bottom. The whole camp was washed; the sand next day looked bright and clean every-where. But that was not all.

Between the dead-line and the stockade, and about half-way between the north gate and the brook, there was a *spring*. It was noticed soon after the storm by some of the boys who lay near by; but they, knowing the ground had always been dry there, thought it was a kind of wet-weather spout, started into life by the big rain. But after a few days, seeing it did not abate, they tied their cups to a tent-pole, and reaching over the dead-line, dipped and drank, and called it the best water in the pen. Others fixed dippers, and soon there was a goodly number there all the time, for a drink of the bright, pure water.

At last some one showed it to the Quartermaster who issued our rations, and interested him in the matter. He gave us boards and nails to make a "V" trough, which we fixed in the spring, and brought the water inside the dead-line.

It yielded about eight or ten gallons per minute of pure, sweet water—much better than could be found in the pen, even by digging for it, before; and till the prison was destroyed, in April, 1865, the flow never diminished. From earliest dawn till far into the night, a crowd was at the spout waiting turn to drink.

The pious thanked God and took courage. The marvelous marveled. The rationalistic advanced two theories: first, the stream had always been there, just under the surface, and being overcharged during the storm, it burst through; second, a discharge of lightning struck there and opened the way to a subterranean reservoir. Why? How?

I care not if lightning or storm is his angel. *God gave us drink!*

CHAPTER VII.

WRECKED.

We received very little reliable news from the outside world. When a squad of new prisoners were brought in they gave us the latest and most reliable news from the department of the army to which they belonged. If the rebels won a victory anywhere, the Quartermaster would bring in a paper at ration time, and read us the account of it, and make us feel as bad as he could. The effect of these reports on the prisoners gave me a chance to study human nature. If he read a report of rebel success in the East, the prisoners from the army of the Potomac were filled with blues and despondency. But if he read an Atlanta paper, that told of a victory in Sherman's department, the Western soldier, in tones of perfect contempt for the whole Confederacy, answered, "Old Bill's leading for your Jack," or he dismissed the subject entirely with, "*It's a —— rebel lie!*"

I think the reason for this was that the Eastern army had been whipped so often that they had learned to expect it; while in Sherman's army, "to fight" and "to whip" were synonymous.

Once in a while we got a fragment of news from the guard. They called the hour of the night and the number of their post, thus:

"P-o-o-ost number one, ten o'clock, and a-a-all's right." "P-o-o-ost number two, ten o'clock, and a-all's right," all around the pen, every hour from dark till daylight. This call was made in a loud, sing-song monotone, that could be heard all over the camp. Sometimes they would interpolate a fragment, thus:

"Post number eight, Lee's falling back,

and all's well." Or, "Post number thirteen, twelve o'clock, and here's your mule."

It was by this means that we first heard of the fall of Atlanta. For two weeks, we Western troops had been full of feverish excitement. That long ago we had read in the Atlanta paper that Sherman had raised the siege, and had fallen back across the Chattahoochee. Every day we begged for more news. The Quartermaster told us that their pickets had been advanced to the river, and Sherman was certainly gone. Scouts had been across, and reported no large body of troops this side of the Kenesaw mountains, and Sherman was doubtless in full retreat on Chattanooga. What could it mean? The rebels evidently believed it, and were rejoicing; we didn't—we *wouldn't*. Still, we were excited; we felt sure that "Old Billy" was playing a deep game, but we wanted to see him "rake the pot."

Then came four or five days of oppressive silence—no news of any kind. We were sure something was being done. But what? How restless and eager we became!

One night the nine o'clock call was started, and ran three posts as usual; but the next was called:

"P-o-ost numbah f-o-a-h, nine o'clock, and Atlanta's gone to ——!"

For one instant the camp was still. In the next, *"Did you hear that?"* Then they cheered. Men got up all over the camp to discuss the news. The midnight call went round long before the camp got quiet again. What if we were hungry, ragged, filthy, and vermin-eaten?—we could be glad. Atlanta was gone!

Early in September the rebs began to move prisoners away from Andersonville. They told us that they were taking us to Charleston to exchange us. But they had told us so many lies of that kind that most of the prisoners did not believe them. They took out two or three train-loads per week.

Four or five train-loads had already gone, when one day Jess M—— (a kinsman of mine) came to me and said that his "ninety" was ordered to be ready to go out that afternoon; and that I could go out with him, on a dead man's name, if I wanted to.

I did not believe the exchange talk; but I did not suppose another pen would be any worse than the one we were in, and as Jess was my only accessible relative, and I loved him as if he were my brother, I decided to go with him.

About four o'clock P. M., a heavy guard marched down to the south gate, and called for the detachments that had been notified that morning. Nine hundred and sixty men were taken out and marched to the depot. There we waited till sundown, when our train backed in. We were put in twelve box cars—*eighty men to a car!* We could not sit or lie. Think of that!—and excuse it who can. Such cruelty is worthy of the period of slave ships, or the men who sailed them.

Two days' rations of corn bread and bacon were put in each car; three companies of guards were distributed over the train, most of them on top of the cars. The officers that were detailed to go took the caboose, and the train started out just as twilight deepened into night.

Where were we going?

It was too dark to see to divide our rations, so we had to let two or three men keep them till morning. We didn't like to, but couldn't help it.

We ran six or seven miles, were running down grade in a cut, when, suddenly, the car seemed to be lifted several feet high, and dropped. It came down with a crash. Part of the timbers of the floor broke upward into the middle of the car, hurling its mass of living freight toward the ends. At the same time two corners were crushed in and two burst outward. For a few seconds there was a loud crashing of timber; then groans, shrieks and wails, and the noise of escaping steam, were the only sounds.

As quick as I could think what had happened, I found myself on top of a squirming, writhing mass of men. A few struggles placed me at an opening made by the outward-bursted corner. I stuck my feet out first, crowded through, and dropped to the ground. I think I was the first man out of our car. The engine lay in the ditch, with its head buried in the bank. The first three cars lay over against the bank just behind it, and were not much damaged. The fourth (the one I was in) lay with one end against the rear of these, and the other end on the track; it having stopped the momentum of the train in that position was what crushed it in the peculiar manner described. The fifth was the worst wreck of all, the sixth having telescoped it from end to end. The forward end of the sixth was crushed in; the rest stood on the track undamaged.

As soon as I felt solid ground beneath my feet, and realized that I was not seriously hurt—the guard were all in confusion and out of place—the thought came to me like an inspiration, "Now is the time to escape! Run for life!"

I started on the impulse, almost without thinking. I rushed past the engine into the darkness. I must have run one hundred yards; I knew I was outside the guard. The moans of the dying and shrieks of the wounded sounded a good distance off.

Then came the thought, "You are leaving Jess. He may be killed or crippled in the wreck." I hesitated—stopped short. I was not willing to go on without Jess, or at least a knowledge of his fate. I ran back. Men were getting out of all the cars. I reached ours, and called. He answered from under the car, and came out.

"Jess, are you hurt?"

"No."

I whispered in his ear, "Let's run off."

He answered, "We couldn't get away. They would catch us."

"Yes we can. There isn't a guard on duty."

Well," said he, "they will bring out the hounds in the morning, and track us up."

"*Nevermind* the hounds!"

I will say for the general reader, that soldiers usually pronounced "never mind" as a word of one syllable, accented all the way through.

I was excited, nervous, vexed, impatient. I felt like every minute was worth a lifetime. Jess was trying to get hold of the meat that had not been divided. That was what he was doing under the car when I came up. He seemed so indifferent, that I said to him:

"If you won't go, I will go alone!"

"All right," said he; "wait a minute and I'll get you a piece of meat."

He went under the car and soon returned with a good piece of bacon. I took it and started. But alas! while I dallied with Jess, the guard recovered from its panic, and had formed a line around the wreck. Just below the engine I was halted and ordered back.

My disappointment was hard to bear. Oh, how I wished that I had kept on when I was free, and had left Jess to his fate!

I went back to the wreck, and went to work with all my might to help rescue the maimed and dead from the debris. We took out ninety-eight Yanks and twenty-four rebs, who were badly wounded, and twenty-six Yanks and eight rebs, dead; a total of thirty-four killed, and one hundred and twenty-two badly hurt.

Such a disaster, in time of peace, would fill with horror the whole country; and yet I doubt if a score of our vast army of readers ever heard of this accident before. I am of the opinion that this is the first time the history of that wreck has ever been in print.

CHAPTER VIII.

PLANS OF ESCAPE.

Rebels and Yanks worked together till the wounded were all out of the wreck, which was probably about midnight. We did not get all the dead out till daylight next morning.

A construction train came down next morning, unloaded its gang of men, took up the wounded, and returned to Andersonville. It returned about noon, and after getting the debris out of the way, and getting all the cars that could be run on the track, they took us back to the pen.

One of the smashed cars was covered with

a tin roof, of which I secured a piece about 20x24 inches, and after getting into prison, I made me a nice pan, by turning up about four inches all around. It proved to be a very valuable piece of property after we began to draw our rations.

When the train came back after taking the wounded, they brought the bloodhounds and took a circuit around the wreck before we left. This gave Jess the exquisite happiness of saying, "*I told you so!*"

Of course, in such a crowd, there were always men studying plans of escape. When the camp was new, and only one stockade stood between the prisoner and freedom, there were many attempts to tunnel out. To do this required much caution and labor. A well was dug about eight or ten feet deep, and from the bottom of this a tunnel was run horizontally to pass under the wall, and then rise to the surface. The work had to be done by night, and the hole kept hid by day. The best tools that we could obtain were a case-knife and half of an unsoldered canteen for digging, and a haversack to carry out the dirt. A good substitute for the haversack, and one often used, was a pants-leg tied up at one end. To prevent caving in, the hole was made as small as possible—I think about twenty inches in diameter, just large enough for a man to crawl through.

After a tunnel was well under way, a man with such an outfit, with two strings to his sack as long as the tunnel, would, by feet and elbows, work his way to the end of the hole, pick the dirt loose with his knife, and with the half canteen scrape it into the sack; then a comrade at the mouth would pull the sack along by one string, he keeping the end of the other to pull it back. A third man would take the dirt away in another sack, pants-leg or blouse-sleeve, and scatter it where it would not be noticed.

A man could hardly get his breath in the tunnel; and owing to the sandy nature of the ground, there was always danger of caving in.

It was hard to keep it secret, for there were men in the pen mean enough to tell the rebels of any such attempt. There was a fellow (he died at Savannah) who wore a large "T" on his forehead. He informed on a tunnel company when they were nearly through, and they made the "T" with a hot railroad spike. After that, when a sneak reported on his fellow-prisoners, the rebs took him out of the pen, and we saw him no more.

If all these dangers and difficulties were surmounted, and the tunnel was opened, the rebs would find the hole the next day, and start the bloodhounds from it.

Oh, those hounds! How we dreaded them! Let the beasts once catch the scent of a poor fugitive, and he was "gone up."

After the outer stockade was built, it greatly increased the difficulty of tunneling, as it would require a length of about two hundred and twenty-five feet to safely pass under both walls. Still there were men desperate enough to attempt it.

One company, after weeks of toil and danger, on a rainy night in August, opened their hole, and crawled to the outer world. I think there were fifteen or twenty went through, though there were so many conflicting reports that I do not pretend to give exact numbers.

The gang of Johnnies that came every morning to count the nineties, found the deficit and reported it. We were notified from headquarters that we would get no rations till those men were found. We did not believe it; we thought it was done to scare us. We only got one scanty little feed each day anyhow, and we didn't think we could live if we missed that. As the hour when they fed us drew near, thousands of hungry men watched the gate. The hour passed. What terrible suspense as the next hour dragged along! Slowly the sun went down behind the dark pines. I thought I would try to describe our feelings as that day went out; but I can't. I shall not try it. I have no words. I give you the bare fact—thirty thousand men, already in a starving condition, fasted forty-eight hours to gratify the malice of those officers, because fifteen or twenty men had outwitted them.

The next day they were brought back,

some of them badly torn and mangled by the bloodhounds.

There were some other plans of escape tried, but they were almost invariably failures, and are not worth mention. I did refer to one—the man who was taken out as dead.

There was a drummer boy, whose smooth face and childish voice called for sympathy. He was rapidly wasting away, and his friends were anxious to save him. The beans were brought in barrels, which were set on the ground to be emptied, and the empty barrels taken out in the last wagon that came in. One day a barrel was turned over on its side to scrape out all the beans; the boy squatted at its mouth, and when the Quartermaster's back was turned, it was turned bottom-upward over him. When the last load came in, two men set that barrel up in the wagon without turning it over. The boy got out all right, but was caught and brought back next day. He didn't last long after that. Three or four weeks later, he was put in a wagon at the other gate. That time we knew that he would never be sent back.

My experience the night of the wreck set me thinking. I knew it was next to impossible to get away from the pen. But they would probably ship more prisoners away. Could a man jump from a train and escape? I believed it could be done. That thought once in my mind, stayed there.

I hunted up several men who, at sundry times and in divers manners, had tried to reach our lines and failed. From them I learned of the dangers to be encountered after getting out.

The South lived in a constant dread of a slave insurrection, and to guard against it the whole country was kept under vigilant surveillance.

If a stranger was seen, he was at once arrested, and made to account for himself. At night the roads were all patrolled by mounted provost guards. A man to be safe, would have to keep well hid by day, and keep away from all traveled roads at night. To travel four or five hundred miles and comply with these conditions is a bigger job than it looks to be till you have worked at it for a week or two. The question of subsistence makes the problem still harder.

After getting all the knowledge and hints I could, I told Cudge S., and asked him to go with me. He would not risk it. I tried Tom B. He heard my plan, and gave me his hand on it.

Our plan was to be taken out, if possible, so as to leave in the evening, so that night would be on the first part of the road; to jump off at some point before we reached Macon; then to travel northwest until we reached the Chattahoochee, and reached the high mountainous divide between it and the waters of the Tombigbee; thence north till we would reach our lines, somewhere between Big Shanty and Resaca.

We expected a four hundred miles trip, and thought we could make it in a month. We expected to keep hid by day till we reached the wooded hills of Alabama, when we hoped to be able to travel a little by day.

CHAPTER IX.

A LEAP FOR FREEDOM.

About the first of October Tom and I found the opportunity to suit us. The train was loaded and guarded about as the wrecked one. We received two days' rations—a piece of corn bread about the size of a brick to each man—no meat this time. Only one guard in our car, and four or five on top.

If was about eleven o'clock. The train was running ten or twelve miles per hour. The men were quarreling, growling and swearing because they were too weak and tired to stand, and had not room enough to lie down. The guard had braced himself against one side of the open door. There were no lights on the train except on the engine and caboose. All the rest was dark as any other freight train. Tom and I worked ourselves over close to the door. We stood and looked out at the star-light night. We tried to seem indifferent, and growled for room, like the rest. But I felt strangely depressed. Some demon of cowardice would keep whispering to me: "You will probably dash your brains out; or you will be seen by the guard and shot to death; or may be you will only break a few bones, so you can't get away, and you will linger and die a cripple, and your friends will never know what has become of you."

These dark probabilities would keep presenting themselves, and I had to fight them back. Finally we sat down in the door. We put our feet out—then drew them in, and squatted there; then hung them out again. We talked of many things to those next to us; but all the time we *thought* of only one thing. We were sitting side by side on the floor, with our feet hanging out at the door.

The guard saw us, but paid no attention. He doubtless thought we had more sense than to jump off a running train. We ran into a cut twelve or fifteen feet deep. It was dark. I nudged Tom. He nodded. I put my hands on the edge of the floor and dropped off. I struck in the ditch. The motion of the train hurled me violently against the ground, but it was soft mud and water. I lay very still till the train went by. When it got two or three hundred yards up the road I got up. I was not hurt. All those presentiments of danger had miscarried. My feelings arose accordingly. I was sure now that I would reach our lines. I walked along the railroad in the direction the train had gone. Tom was about two hundred yards from where I fell. I asked why he didn't jump out sooner. He said the train seemed to him to go faster after I jumped. He fell on harder ground, and had bruised his shoulder.

We climbed out of the cut, sat on the fence, and looked at the north star— that friend universal of wandering man. Now for four hundred miles of star-light walking, bearing ever a little west of that star. Tom had a pair of miserable old boots. I was barefooted. We each had a blouse and pants in tolerable preservation. Our shirts were worn out. We had no baggage, no tools—not even a pocket-knife. *We were outlaws.* Not a crime in the catalogue would so surely alienate us from everybody and debar us from sympathy, as the fact that we were U. S. soldiers in Dixie.

We jumped off the fence and started. Our hearts were stout, if our legs were a little shaky. We traveled across corn and cotton fields till gray light streaked the eastern horizon, then entered a thicket, and as it grew light we worked our way into it. It proved to be a large cypress swamp, surrounded by a dense thicket. By the edge of the oozy swamp we broke off twigs and branches of trees, and made us a bed, and as the sun mounted up the sky, we stretched our weary limbs and slept.

We agreed to watch and sleep by turns; but I think the watcher slept as soundly as the sleeper. The one thing we dreaded was the possibility of prowling hounds tracking us up and calling attention to us by their bark; but here we felt safe, for on a log, not more than fifty feet away in the swamp, lay an alligator about ten feet long, and we knew no hound would care to hunt along the shore of that swamp. The reptile lay there for two hours about the middle of the day, and we regarded him as a friend, although we did not desire any closer intimacy.

In the afternoon we ate one ration of our bread, and before the sun went down we worked our way through the jungle to its northwest end; from which, as soon as it grew dark, we again set forth on our journey, crossing, fields, woods, roads and streams. We traveled quietly. When we came onto a road, we stopped, listened, and if we heard no sound we crossed it quickly. Even if it ran our course we would not follow it, for fear of meeting a patrolman.

During this second night we came onto a field of sweet potatoes. We dug and ate some of them, and put some in our blouse pockets for next day. We traveled well that night, going probably twenty miles; but before day we ran into a swamp on our track, and being tired, we stopped and waited for light, when we worked into it, and spent the second day much as we did our first. We ate the last of our bread and as much new sweet potato as we dared.

The third night we had a hard time. Our course lay mostly through woods, and we ran into three or four swamps, and had to make wide detours to pass around them. We did not make many miles headway that night. The next day we were still in such thickets and forests, and after sleeping three or four hours we traveled in daylight, moving cautiously, and keeping well under cover of the thickets, as we slipped along. We came across a tree full of ripe persimmons, and ate a large mess

There is a good deal of food in this fruit. It satisfied our hunger and strengthened us. I think I never enjoyed a meal more. We kept on till the sound of chopping wood and the crowing of fowls warned us that we were approaching an inhabited country when we hid in the bushes and waited for the friendly darkness to renew our journey. The fourth night we passed so close to a house that the dogs barked at us, and we ran our best away from it. We were again bothered by swamps. About midnight we ran into one, backed out, flanked to the right about half a mile, and tried again. Couldn't make it. Went a half mile farther, and again failed.

CHAPTER X.

IN THE SWAMPS.

While we were making efforts to flank the swamp, the sky was overcast with clouds. It became so dark that we could not see at all, so we were compelled to stop. We felt around in the dark and ran against a large tree, at the root of which we reclined and waited for day.

As the darkness began to turn to a leaden gray, it began to rain. Slowly and in small drops at first, but soon gaining till it rained hard. All the leaves were dripping, and we were soaked and chilled in a short time;

and yet the rain showed no sign of quitting.

We took the blues and grumbled, murmured and were on the point of quarreling with each other. Everything was wrong. We had not found a thing to eat all night—had no hope of finding anything in that jungle; and if the rain and clouds continued we could not leave it the coming night, for we would have no guide for our course unless the sun or stars should appear, and by the next morning we would probably be too weak to walk.

When Elijah ran into the wilderness to escape the idolatrous Jezebel, *he* took the blues, and thought he had better be dead. Instead of reasoning with him, *God fed him*. And while Tom and I sat dripping, chilled and empty in that swamp, I think our despondency belonged more to our physical than to our mental condition.

As we reclined at the root of the tree, a large green frog came hopping through the wet leaves and moss. We did not philosophize and draw a lesson from his progress, as the Tartar chieftain did from the ant;

neither did we draw the Christian's lesson of trust, that if God feeds the frog in the jungle, he will care for us. But Tom said, "let's have him," and falling his length, covered the reptile with his broad palm. To divide him with our thumb nails was the work of an instant; to eat him took but a minute more. There were no fragments to be taken up after the meal.

One frog could not satisfy our appetite, but it stopped the gnawing of the stomach and the ringing in the head. We liked it.

The rain ceased, and after noon the sun appeared occasionally through the clouds. We flanked the swamp, waded a wide, sluggish creek, waist deep, and worked through a canebrake before night.

We came to a cornfield, and about sundown we climbed the fence. The corn had been gathered, but we searched till we found one ear that had been missed, which we ate. We found some dry beans also among the cornstalks, and ate a few of them, but they were not palatable in their new state, and, as we had no means to cook them, we ate but few.

We crossed corn and cotton fields that night, following the rows to keep from being turned from our course, as the stars did not show. We estimated the distance across these fields at four miles. The country was level, and the fields were muddy from the rain; so, by the time we had crossed them and run into a canebrake on the west side, we were tired enough to lie down.

The next morning was foggy, and stands out in memory as eminently *the* morning that we fought gallinippers. That pest of the swamp seemed determined to take what little blood we had, and we fought to save it.

After a while the fog floated off, and the sun shone brightly. We picked a place and lay in the sun till we dried our clothes, which had been wet for twenty-four hours.

On the other side of this canebrake was a cornfield, in which we found three or four ears, and ate a good mess. We followed the cane to where it merged into a thicket, in which we found wild grapes. This thicket was in a narrow slough running between cleared fields. It was not more than fifty yards wide. While we were gathering the grapes we heard a gun not very far away. We crept into the thickest bushes near, and lay flat on the ground. Soon a man, carrying a gun, passed along the edge of the field, not more than twenty yards from us. He was the first human being we had seen since we left the train. The sight made us nervous for awhile; but after hearing two shots a good distance up the thicket, and waiting awhile, we crept out and continued our journey down the slough.

Traveling in a thicket is slow work,—creeping under, climbing over, crowding through the vine-tied bushes. But we kept at it till all at once we stood on the bank of a broad, smooth-flowing river.

What river is it? We ransacked our meager knowledge of Georgia geography. It must be Flint River; and yet if it is, we are not where we thought we were. We had not been carried as far by rail as we thought. It was Flint River.

One thing was certain: the river lay in our way, and must be crossed; and we thought it best to prepare to cross before dark. The banks were lined with birch and cane. We started up stream under cover of this growth, hunting for driftwood to build a raft. We found a little path, and followed it till it turned down the bank. There we found an old dug-out, or log canoe, chained to a tree and locked.

We waited patiently for twilight to settle over river and timber. I found a piece of clapboard for a paddle. Tom took a stake and pried out the staple that fastened the chain to the boat. The owner doubtless found his lock and chain all right, but his canoe was like the dog whose master tied him to the rear car, thinking he could trot along behind the train.

CHAPTER XI.

BLOODHOUNDS.

We crossed Flint River, turned the boat loose, for fear of being tracked from it by hounds, struggled up the bank, and toiled through a dense thicket. The ground was low and had been washed by floods. The old growth of cane and willow had been washed down and stood at a slight angle from the ground, and the new had grown up through it. Imagine a lapped willow hedge, covering acres of ground, with two men going through it in the dark, and you have a true picture.

After working through the tow-head for

thirty or forty rods, we found we were on an island. Our boat was gone. There was nothing with which to make a raft. We had crossed the main stream, but before us was a channel sixty or eighty feet wide, and of unknown depth.

I have known theologians to discuss, the question, "Who has a right to pray?" I think it is one of the natural rights; and that any one in mental health does pray sometimes. He needs revelation to acquaint him with the Being he addresses, but he will pray whether he knows Him or not.

If any one doubts my theory, swimming a river where alligators abound is a good way to test it. Here's a chance for Tyndall. As we plunged into the dark waters, our souls cried out to the Invisible One, not in audible words, but in earnest breathings. I'll never forget it. We knew such channels were favorite resorts for these monsters, and that one crash of their powerful jaws would end at once our sufferings and our hopes.

Across. Up the bank; through a thicket. A fence, and broad meadows beyond. We pulled off our clothes, rung out the water, and put them on again. But I fear I will weary the reader with these details. "Prison life," in which thousands were involved with me, has dwindled down to a personal narrative, and I will not bore you by asking you to go over the whole course of our wanderings.

We kept on our course by night, and hid by day. When we could find nothing to eat in the fields, we were forced to try at negro cabins, to beg of their scanty fare.

When this had to be done, one went alone, and the other hid, with this understanding that if the one who went was captured, he should tell that he was traveling alone; and the other, after waiting a reasonable time, should go on by himself. I went once, and Tom twice. He came near getting caught one time while waiting for a hoe-cake to bake. The overseer came to the cabin where he was, and he was covered up in a pile of rags in the corner.

In crossing fields, we often encountered a low-running briar, called dewberry vines. My bare feet and ankles were soon badly scratched, and full of thorns, and going through the weeds and fens were poisoned. During the day they would swell up, and were very feverish. When I would start out in the evening, it was like walking on a boil for a mile or two. I would sweat and shake with the pain, and it required a strong effort of the will to go on at all. After a mile or so they would get numb, and I would get along better; unless I tore them afresh on the briars. In the morning they would throb and ache, and swell again.

A new trouble stared us in the face after we had been out ten or twelve days—Tom was failing. He was about six feet high, and well proportioned. In our lines, he would weigh about one hundred and eighty. Of course it required more food to keep him than a smaller man. He never complained. He was too gritty for that. But at almost every fence we crossed he would say, "Oats, let's rest a little." During the day he had aching in his bones and head; his eyes were deeply sunken in their sockets, and he could get but little sleep. He would sit for hours with his elbows on his knees and his chin in his hands. After looking at him, his haggard face and hollow black eyes would stay in my mind when I turned away, and I could not help asking the question: "Will he last long enough to reach home?" or, "If he fails and gets down, what can I do for him?" I could see but two courses to choose from, in such an event—one was to go to the nearest house and surrender us up. The other, to make him a bed in the thicket, and forage by night, and watch him by day, till he mended or died. He did not get down, but kept on till we had been out fifteen nights. During that time we had traveled about one hundred and fifty miles—an average of ten miles per night.

At this time General Hood had started on his Nashville campaign, and his Georgia soldiers were deserting in great numbers. The Provost Marshals were ordered to hunt them up and return them to their commands.

Their plan for executing this order was, to warn the citizens against feeding or helping the deserters in any way; and in case any one was found about their premises, they were ordered to notify the Marshal at once, so that he could go and arrest them.

We spent the fourteenth day of our pilgrimage in a little thicket on the border of a large plantation. It was not a swamp, but a patch of briars and brambles allowed to grow along the fence, because of the slovenly method of farming. We felt uneasy on account of the insecurity of our hiding-place, and did not dare to move about in search of food, lest we expose ourselves. So we kept still and fasted till dark. When night came we started, determined to hunt food, and make what headway we could. But we had fasted so long that we staggered like drunken men, and that terrible ringing of the head warned us that we must find food or go crazy before long.

Failing in the fields, we approached the negro quarters of the plantation. We aroused the inmates of two or three cabins, and begged, but got nothing. They said they had nothing. My opinion is, that they did not believe we were genuine Yanks, and were afraid to help us. Finally, we found an old darkey who said his wife cooked for the white folks, and that if we would slip around into the kitchen behind the mansion, we could get something to eat. He told us how to get in, and how to find the pantry stores. We wanted him to go and bring us out something, but he refused. There it was, and we could get it ourselves if we wanted it. We sat down in the dark shadow of the fence, and quietly discussed the chances of starving or getting food elsewhere. It was several miles to another plantation. We decided that this was our best chance; and cautiously approached and silently entered the kitchen. We followed the negro's directions, and found bread, meat and milk. We drank the milk, and taking a piece of bread and meat in our hands, we "silently stole away."

We traveled three or four miles. The ringing in our heads gradually ceased, but our limbs wabbled badly all night. Before day we found a little thicket in the midst of a cotton field, and decided to halt and make it our hiding-place for the next day. So ended the fifteenth and last night of our flight.

From the night that we jumped off the cars till we, all damp with the night's dews, crept into this thicket, our hope had grown higher and higher. Every thicket where we made our lair for a day—yes, every field we crossed, seemed to make our prospect brighter. "*If* we reach our lines" was gradually changing to "*When* we reach our lines," in our thought and conversation. It was still a long way off, but we would not be likely to meet worse obstacles than we had already encountered; and if our strength only held out, we would make it by and by. This was the way we felt on the morning after this nights adventure.

About midday we were sitting in a sunny spot in the thicket, trying to get warm enough to make us sleepy.

Tom was sitting, or squatting, a few feet from me, hugging his knees and resting his chin in his hands. I was reclining against some bushes that I had bent down. Neither had spoken for some time.

My ear caught a sound. I listened. Presently I heard it again a little plainer. I raised up and sat erect, all attention. Yes, I could hear it better now. Every nerve was strained to listen. The blood seemed to all rush into my heart—my heart into my throat. I shuddered, and turned sick. I had heard that sound before. It was often borne to our ears as we lay in Andersonville; especially on the day after the tunnel was opened.

I looked at Tom. He had not changed his position, but his great black eyes were glaring at me with a wild, hopeless expression in them.

"Tom, do you hear those hounds?"

"They are on our track!"

"What shall we do?"

"What *can* we do!"

Sure, enough! What could we do in our condition? If we had only had our carbines we might have done something. But we had nothing—not even a knife.

The brutes were getting closer. They

CAPTURED BY BLOODHOUNDS.

were coming across the field toward our thicket. We climbed a tree.

Five men, armed and mounted, and four bloodhounds soon discovered us. They ordered us to surrender; called off the hounds, and we came down.

The Provost Captain of this squad looked us all over, and said:

"Who the —— are you?"

We told him. He was looking for deserters, and was as much surprised at finding Yanks in that part of the country as we were at being found. But somehow he enjoyed the surprise much better than we.

To us it was terrible. All our risk, our toil, our suffering, had come to nothing. When we learned that we would be sent back to Andersonville, Tom begged the guard to shoot him, and end his misery at once.

I felt very much as Tom did. Neither of us thought that we could live through the winter in that pen. Hope was dead. Despair settled down upon us. I cannot describe it. No one who has not felt it would recognize the picture. May God preserve the reader from ever knowing by experience the meaning of the word.

CHAPTER XII.

WANTED—A SHIRT.

The captain of the squad that caught us was a good-natured, jolly old fellow, who looked as though he lived on the best beef and brandy in Georgia. He treated us well.

They stopped with us, after dark, at the house of a wealthy planter, in the northern part of Talbott county—a large, white house, in a grove of oaks. It looked pretty and homelike in the moonlight, as we entered the yard. We saw none of the family that night except the host, a pleasant old gentleman, with white hair and beard. He listened with interest to the captain's account of our capture, and asked us a number of questions. He made the servants prepare supper for the guard and us; and told us that we were welcome to all we could eat, but advised us to be careful not to eat too much. He then ordered beds prepared for the whole party. Tom and I told him we were not fit to sleep in a bed, but he insisted; so we washed and went to bed. A fire was built in our room, and the four rebel soldiers divided the time so that two of them were on guard by the fire all night.

I have often thought of their careful watch. We were weary, foot-sore and thoroughly discouraged. With a fair start we could not make over five or six miles that night, and with their hounds they could catch us by ten o'clock next day. If they had put their guns where we could not get hold of them, I don't think we would have tried to get away. Yet such was their caution that they sat up by twos to guard us.

We did not sleep much. We were too blue. Our future looked dark. I was nervous and wakeful, and as Tom tossed about in the bed, deep sighs, that were almost sobs, told me that he could not sleep.

In the morning after we were up and washed, our host came in, and, with Southern hospitality, set before us a big black bottle, a sugar-bowl, and tumblers. The bottle contained a fiery liquor, called by the Johnnies in those days, "sanguin."

Tell the Temperance Reformer to go on with his crusade. May God speed him in his efforts. He is right—it *was* vile stuff. Our host knew it, but he apologized by saying that the accursed Yankee blockade had cut off his supply of old Kentucky Bourbon, and he offered us the best he had.

He then led us and our guard out to breakfast. It had been a long, long time since Tom or I had sat at table with ladies. Even in our lines, in campaign from Chattanooga to Atlanta, we had no such privileges. As we entered the dining room the host gave us some sort of a general introduction to three ladies—his wife and daughters. It is fashionable for men to accuse the other sex of vanity; but we have our full share.

When I looked across the table at those well-dressed ladies, and down at my tattered pants, and swollen, discolored feet, I felt bashful and awkward; and as I drew my blouse more closely about my neck and breast, the desire for giddy display so overcame me that for one brief moment I wished I had a shirt. I sat down embarrassed by the feeling that I was not fit to be there. But the table talk turned at once upon the war and its current campaigns, and the boastful manner in which they spoke of the prowess of their armies, and the skill of their generals, soon aroused my combativeness and put me at my ease.

Their greatest boast was the skill of General Hood. He had flanked the flanker; he had gone around Sherman; had got between him and his best general (Thomas), and could now strike either way. Sherman's only chance of escape would be to break up his army into small divisions and go out through East Tennessee. To one who remembers the campaign of 1864, in which Thomas fell back before Hood till he got everything ready, and then utterly

"FOR ONE BRIEF MOMENT I WISHED I HAD A SHIRT."

crushed the life out of his army, this boasting has its moral.

Of course Tom and I entered into the discussion—much of it was addressed to us. They charged many hard things against the U. S. Government. Some of them we denied, some we could defend, and some we couldn't.

They said we could never whip them in the world. We said the United States would govern the country or make a wilderness of it, and we didn't care which.

We spoke bitterly of Andersonville, and told them—and we thought so then—that we could not live through the coming winter if they sent us back there, and we hoped our Government would retaliate. That if we could be sure that for every man who languished in Andersonville one would freeze in Camp Douglass, we would go and bravely die and rot there. We were *not a bit* excited. Only earnest and warm. May be it was the "sanguin" juice.

One standard subject for hard feeling in those days was the enlistment of the negro into the army. It was seldom that we ever got into a discussion with the rebels that they did not refer to that. One of the soldiers present said: "Yo Gove'ment thinks you-alls no bettah than niggahs, foh it puts niggahs in yo ahmy,"—and he looked at the ladies for approval. One of us retorted: "Then your Government thinks you are no better than hounds, for it uses hounds for the same purpose!"

So we had it up and down during the entire breakfast. The old captain allowed us full freedom of speech, if not of person, and we indulged ourselves. I have given these hard speeches and ruffled feelings thus fully because of what followed.

After breakfast was over, while the provost were getting ready to start with us, the mistress of the house gave Tom and me an old quilt to be owned in common, a small sack filled with provisions for us to eat on the way, and to each of us a pair of home-spun and home-knitted cotton socks.

I felt as though I could not take the gifts, after all that had passed, and I told the woman, "Madam, we are here as your enemies. We have lodged under your roof because we could not help ourselves. Let us part as enemies. Our strongest desire is that we may live to be reunited with our regiment, that we may raid through this country and make war terrible to it. Don't make us feel that we are under obligations to a human being in this whole land."

She answered: "I have two boys, soldiers with Lee in the army of Virginia. If they should ever be captured and brought to your mother, so destitute as you are, I would want her to do something for them, and I want to do something for you. Our own army has made so many requisitions on us that there is but little left that I could spare. I would like to give you some warm clothing, but I have none. This quilt may afford some shelter from the wintry winds, and these socks will be some protection to your feet. You won't refuse them?"

I bit my under lip. I bit my upper lip—it was no use—the tears would come. I couldn't help it. I could answer taunt with taunt; but kindness found every picket asleep. I was surprised. There was something in my throat I could not swallow. That woman's Christianity cropped out above her patriotism. Be patient, reader, and let me linger a little. It is the only bright spot in all those dreary months.

My memory of prison life is a dark, sluggish lagoon, with muddy banks and oozy bed, from which all beauty has departed. But look! Rising from the black water and floating on the scummy surface, we found a lovely water-lily, mingling its sweet perfume with the pestilential vapors. As I look back over my life, I see no one deed that moved its currents more deeply than this one.

I hope that that woman received her boys safe and sound at the end of the war.

CHAPTER XIII.

JAILED.

We put on the socks. I told the woman I would never forget her kindness, and so far I have kept my promise. That was October 20th, 1864—just sixteen years ago. During these years I have changed so much that I can hardly identify myself; and I think that no one who knows the preacher of to-day, would recognize in him the reckless, hopeless "Oats" of that day; and still the events of that morning are as vivid in my memory as though they had happened during the last year.

The guard ordered us to start. The captain and one soldier went with us. They were mounted, and ordered us to walk before them. The road was dusty; in places, rough; and they kept urging us to walk faster, until we were almost exhausted.

Toward noon we came to Talbotton, the county-seat. I can describe it with one sentence: The railroad missed it. I think you can all see its general dilapidation in that sentence.

We came to the public square, and were stopped under a large shade tree. *Two Yanks in town!* The news spread rapidly, and soon brought around us a crowd of ladies (?) and gentlemen (?). Everybody seemed to be at leisure. No, we did not feel proud of our notoriety. A dog-fight would have called the same crowd together.

They bemeaned us, and berated us soundly, and when we told them that we were Kentuckians, they became more abusive still. They could overlook the meanness of New England Yanks, but Kentucky Yanks were *traitors*, and ought to be hung! The ladies (?) used the most insulting language at their command.

Finally, an old man, with long, white beard, a harsh, cracked voice, and an extraordinary vocabulary of profane and vulgar language, spoke thus:

"I'd hang 'em! String 'em up! I wouldn't guard such. Give 'em hemp!"

Tom turned on him like the caged lion that he was:

"You'd hang 'em? I believe you. It's just your pluck! Hang two *miserable, starved, sick prisoners!* You're a brave! You never saw a real, live Yank. You coward! Go up to Atlanta and see them with the horns on. If you heard the Yanks were coming this way you'd run and hide!"

I give the substance of these speeches as well as I can. To report them in full would require the use of a good many words that are spelled "———" in polite literature.

Tom's speech fired the whole crowd. It was a regular mob, and they began to talk earnestly about doing what the old man suggested. Our old captain had left us in charge of the guard for a short time; but he rode up just in time, and with a cocked pistol in his hand, threatened to shoot the first man who tried to molest us. He ordered us to keep our mouths shut, and said if we wouldn't talk so saucy there would be no danger.

I was scared. When I was captured the day before, I thought I would as lief be shot. But when I looked in the face of death at the hands of that mob, I found I did not want to die in that way—then.

A new guard, one man, was detailed to take us on to Geneva. He drove us before him down the road. We were very tired and weak. We begged him to let us rest; but he was in a hurry. Finally, a man in a spring-wagon overtook us, and the guard had him haul us. He was a kind man, and the first Southerner we had found who thought there was any possibility of Hood having made a mistake in his campaign. He freely admitted that he did not see the wisdom of leaving Sherman in Atlanta with sixty thousand men, and not even a decent skirmish line between him and the heart of Georgia.

"They were fools if they thought he would stay where they wanted him to, till Hood got ready to come back and whip him!"

Ah! how Tom and I enjoyed this chat. It was more delicious than nectar. It would beat sorghum juice!

Geneva is a town on the Macon & Columbus railroad. Our friend with the buggy took us to the depot, and as he left, gave us two dollars (Confed.) apiece to buy tobacco with. We passed a resolution, by a standing vote, that he was "Bully!"

We were put on a train and taken to Columbus, Georgia, where we arrived a little before dark. Columbus was at that time a thrifty-looking little city. We had not gone far till we saw a familiar face on the other side of the street—the face of a wooden Indian. The guard crossed over, and we invested our "Confed." in "Ole Virginny." We were then taken to military headquarters.

Every old soldier remembers the unspeakable contempt in which we used to hold these red-tape fops, who always kept out of danger by being detailed on post duty in the rear. You remember we used to have a name for them. *Sycophant* is as near the meaning of the word as any term I can find, but that is not quite the word that we used. It will doubtless help us to forgive the rebel soldiers to know that they were cursed by the same class of dandies in their rear.

At headquarters in Columbus we found two or three of these fops. Our guard approached one who was writing at a desk, and, saluting him, began:

"I have two prisoners—"

"I ain't the man."

He crossed the room to the other desk, and again began his statement. The clerk spoke in a haughty, disdainful manner—

"Where did you get these men?"

"Capt. —— caught them near ——."

"Where did they come from?"

"They say, from Andersonville."

"Too many men get out of Andersonville," as though the guard could help it. He then turned and looked at us with as much contempt in his glance as a hotel clerk would give to a Congressman, and asked:

"How did you get out?"

"We climbed out on a grape-vine."

He wrote a little note and handed it to the guard.

"Take these men to jail, and give that to the jailer." So we went to jail in the city of Columbus, Georgia.

We were criminals! Our crime was believing in the Government of the United States, and being willing to defend its flag.

CHAPTER XIV.

CAMP LAWTON.

The jail at Columbus was an iron building. It consisted of a hall about twelve feet wide, twenty feet long, and twelve feet high; with a double tier of cells on each side. Each cell was about six feet cube. A shelf about two feet wide ran along each side of the hall, six feet from the floor, by which we had access to the upper tier of cells. In each cell was a kind of bunk or shelf to sleep on.

When Tom and I were turned into that jail, there were seventeen jail-birds there.

I remember the number seventeen, but am not sure whether there were seventeen before we entered, or whether we made the number.

One man—a murderer—was kept locked in his cell. All the rest of us stayed in the common hall by day, and slept in the cells, or on the hall floor by night, as we pleased.

We were a select company. One old man was there for dodging the conscript law. There were two deserters from the rebel army, waiting until they could be forwarded to their command. There were two roughs who were sent there for raising a row in a brothel down town. A Texan, for killing a quartermaster. Three negroes; two of them for trying to run off. I can't remember all of them, but last, as the chief of criminals, Tom and I—two Yanks!

We were there ten or twelve days. I don't remember the exact time; but it was a good place to stay. We had two good meals per day, consisting of good corn bread (not the Andersonville kind), bacon, cabbage, rice, etc., all well cooked and enough of it. One of the negroes had friends outside who brought him peanuts, which he shared with us; and the roughs had "friends" of their kind, who brought them delicacies, and when they learned that there were Yanks in there, they gave us oranges.

We improved in health, strength, and spirits, rapidly; and we passed another resolution by a large majority: Whereas, we have to be prisoners; Resolved—That we would rather be treated as *criminals* than as prisoners of war! And I now record that resolution in these minutes.

The blessings of this world are transient, and sooner or later we have to give them up. The Columbus jail was not an exception. About two hundred prisoners, captured by Hood at Atlanta, Georgia, were being forwarded to prison by way of Columbus. When they arrived, our jailer was ordered to put us with them.

We were taken out of jail in the evening, and put with the other prisoners, who were corralled on a vacant lot and closely guarded. The next morning we were loaded on a train of flat cars and taken to Macon.

Tom was feeling well, and my feet were in a fair way to recover. Hood was about Chattanooga, so we decided that if we run that night we would jump off, and aim to go straight to Atlanta. The reader may try to imagine our disappoint when, instead of going on, they took us off the cars at Macon, and again put us in camp. We saw that they did not intend to travel by night, so we tried to think of some way to run the guard.

We were put in a place that had a high, tight board fence on three sides of it; on the fourth ran the Ocmulgee river. The guards walked around inside of the fence, and along the river bank. Tom conceived the idea of slipping past the guard on the bank, getting down to the water, and quietly swimming and floating with the current out of town. We tried to do it, but the guard was too vigilant, and we had to give it up after narrowly escaping being shot.

The next morning we were again put on the flat cars, and started toward Savannah. Riding on those open flat cars gave us a good chance to see the country, and we made close observations, even counting the streams we crossed. The country was very flat, large swamps were abundant—it looked as if fully half the land was swampy. We saw but few clearings or other indications of an inhabited country. We did not think we could get through such a country by night, but it looked as though there would not be much danger in daylight.

About three o'clock we came to Millen Junction, where the Augusta road intersects the Savannah & Macon railroad. Our train switched off and ran up the Augusta road two or three miles, to where the rebels had established a new prison, called by them, "Camp Lawton," but known to us as the "Millen Prison."

This prison was built on the same general plan as the one at Andersonville, but it was much better every way.

It was a stockade pen, enclosing about twenty-five acres. Wall, sentry-boxes, and dead-line as at Andersonville. The water was clear and comparatively pure, as there was no camp on the creek above the pen. The trees along this creek were left for shade, making probably three acres of timber. The creek went murmuring through this forest shade, following its own winding channel for about half the distance across the pen. From the middle of the pen to the lower stockade the stream was confined in a straight channel about four feet wide, through which it rushed in a way that would carry off all the filth of the prison. A good bridge was built across the creek at the head of this straight part.

The prisoners all stayed on the west side of the stream, and used the grove and the east side as a kind of public park or promenade.

What would we not have given for such an addition to Andersonville, during those horrible hot days in August?

CHAPTER XV.

THE PRESIDENTIAL ELECTION.

Any one can see by my description of Camp Lawton, that it was a better place than Andersonville. Still it lacked a good deal of being a fit place in which to spend the winter.

When Tom and I entered, about the first of November, 1864, there were about ten thousand men there. They were all corralled on the west side of the creek, and were without shelter, except such miserable apologies as we saw in Andersonville.

Nearly all the men in the prison were

from that horrid pen—taken out on *promise of exchange*, only to keep them docile and tractable till they could get them to a safer place.

It is mean to raise hopes and dash them down, and the effect was plainly seen here in the large number in which hope was dead, and who were anxious to be dead literally, as the only way to escape from woes that had become unbearable.

Tom and I wandered about among these miserable wretches till dark, searching for our acquaintances. We found none that day. At night we picked out a place, and spreading our quilt—that woman's gift, we laid us down on the damp ground, under the cold gray mists of a November night. Thousands lay about us who had not even the comfort that we derived from our quilt, but chilled and shook the night away, with nothing but a ragged shirt and pants to shield their starving bodies. We ought to have been thankful, but we were not.

Next day we renewed our search, and found a number of our regiment—among them my partners in the sack tent. As I still owned my share in that fly, and as Tom had found some of his former messmates, we swapped our quilt for a blanket, tore it in halves, and dissolved partnership. We were not tired of each other. We were always friends—more than friends—we were "pards." Get some old soldier to tell you what that means, and you will know how strong was our attachment. We could each get a better shelter by separating; hence we tore the blanket.

The most notable event of our sojourn in this pen was the Presidential election. The rebels furnished us with papers containing extracts from Northern papers calling the war a failure, and saying that if McClellan is elected he will bring it to a close. You who were in the loyal States during that campaign, doubtless understood all the questions at issue. Only one question reached the wretched prisoner in his dreary pen. And that was raised by that plank in the platform on which Little Mc. stood—"Resolved, That *the war is a failure.*"

Rebel officers came in and talked freely

with us, giving it as their opinion that if McClellan was elected, the war would close and we would all be at home before Spring. For this they furnished us abundant proof from the Northern press. As the day of election approached, we became deeply interested, and but little was talked of but the great question at issue and the probable result.

Oh, how anxious we were to go home! To leave all that wretchedness behind! But did we want the questions of the war to fail in order that we could go home?

If Lincoln was elected it meant that the war would go on; that we would probably have to languish in prison for dreary months to come. To many it meant *death by slow torture!*

We became somewhat excited, and determined to vote on the questions ourselves. We knew our vote would not be counted in the returns, but we wanted to know how the prisoners would vote.

We made all needed arrangements to secure a fair election, and when the day came we voted. We had no electors on our tickets, but voted directly for Lincoln and McClellan. I do not remember the exact number of votes cast for each candidate, but it was about eight thousand for Lincoln and fifteen hundred for "Little Mc.," in a camp of ten thousand.

Does the reader of to-day understand that vote? What did it *mean?* What did it *say* to those rebel officers who watched it so closely? It meant that we were willing to chill and starve; to endure the horrors of prison pens; to die, or worse, to become lunatics and idiots if need be, rather than see the war closed with dishonor to the American flag. It said to those rebels, *Do your worst,* we'll never ask *you* for peace.

It says to the historian: You may take at random four names out of five, from the lists of our volunteer soldiers and write them by the side of Marcus Regulus, of immortal fame.

The rebels had counted us in companies of one hundred, for the purpose of issuing rations to us. Each company had a mess sergeant, whose duty it was to call up his hundred, to be counted in the morning, and to draw and divide the rations in the afternoon. We voted by these company hundreds, in this election. Rebel officers were in the pen nearly all the day, watching for the result. But in the afternoon when we began to count the vote, and the "Lincoln hirelings" began to shout, and the "Mudsills" began to sing "The Star-Spangled Banner," "Red, White and Blue," etc., they left in disgust.

I met one, a major, down by the bridge, as he was leaving. I asked him if he was satisfied with the returns. He answered:

"That's yo affah, suh; I don't care how you vote! Jeff Davis is my candidate."— Yet something in his tone did belie his words. We serenaded the guard that night by singing "John Brown."

CHAPTER XVI.

ENLISTMENTS.

When we were in Andersonville there were many attempts to find mechanics and artisans among the prisoners.

Calls were made for shoemakers, machinists, blacksmiths, etc. The rebel authorities offered to furnish food and clothing and pay good wages to any one who would go out on parole and work in their shops. It was a great temptation to mechanics who were starving in filth and rags; and a good many yielded to it and went out. I will say, though, that but few native Americans were among them. They were generally foreigners who did not fully understand the war and its issues.

It was also intimated that if any one would enlist in their army, he would receive rations and pay as a soldier, but while in Andersonville I saw no strong effort to induce any one to enlist. But in Camp Lawton, soon after the Presidential election, rebel recruiting officers came into the pen and openly and boldly tried to hire men to join the rebel army.

They offered any one a good suit and fifty dollars (Confederate) at once, and would take him out and put him on full rations, as soon as he would sign his name to their muster roll.

Winter was rapidly coming. Already its cold, driving rains and a few chilling frosts had reached our wretched abode—if you can call an open field an abode. You need not travel twenty rods to view a thousand naked backs, turning purple in the cold, bleak wind. Our own Government had refused to exchange us. There seemed to be no prospect of escape. The prospect of staying *alive* in there was about as hopeless. Is it strange that they found a few men who were willing to swear allegiance to the Confederacy—with the mental reservation that they would desert as soon as they could?

As I look back across sixteen years at those events, my surprise is, that so few could be found who would go! I forget the exact number, but I think about seventy enlisted at that time. Less than one in a hundred.

After their names had been obtained, a drum beaten at the gate called them out. As they went over the creek toward the gate, thousands—almost the entire camp—crossed over to see them go out; and the miserable wretches had to run a gauntlet of the fiercest hisses and blood-curdling curses that ever saluted mortal ears! And only the presence of a strong rebel guard prevented that vast mob from falling upon them, then and there. Such an hour of fierce excitement leaves its track on the soul for years. To-day, as memory calls it up, my hand trembles under its influence.

About the last of November, the rebel sergeants came into camp just after noon and gave orders to about half the prisoners to get ready to go out that evening. This order threw the camp into the wildest excitement. "Is it an exchange?" "Where are we going?" "Why are we moved?" We pelted the Johnnies with such questions to no purpose. They told us they knew nothing about it. We were all anxious to go. Not only the hundreds that were ordered, but all the rest took down their meager tents and rolled them up, and at sunset the whole camp was massed at the gate, impatiently waiting for it to open.

The first hundred was called. A hundred was counted out. Not the hundred that had messed together; for wherever there was a weak or sick man in the squad, he was unceremoniously crowded out by a stronger man of another hundred. No man said, "by your leave." It was a grand illustration of the "survival of the fittest." Selfishness ruled supreme. Groans, curses and blows mingled, as men struggled to keep in place, or crowded to find one by displacing some one else. Since "Oats" has turned preacher, and is trying to walk in the path of peace, I think I had better not tell in what part of the column he went out.

We were loaded on trains, and run down to Millen Junction, where we remained closely guarded until after midnight. We tried to find out from the guard our destination, but they either did not know or would not tell. After a weary delay they pulled out on the Savannah road, and ran at unusual speed—for a freight train—for thirty or forty miles, when they stopped and went into a sidetrack at a station, in the midst of a dreary, swampy flat, where we remained until daylight.

CHAPTER XVII.

LIFE ON THE RAILROAD.

The next day we rolled along over what seemed to be a great, monotonous plain, as wide and as flat as the broad prairies of Northeastern Illinois or Northern Indiana. The poor, sandy plains were timbered with pitch pine, and where the land became swampy, cypress took the place of the pine. Once in a while we would see a clearing, sometimes quite a large plantation, but more than nine-tenths of the land was covered by the primitive forest, almost as wild as when the Creeks and Cherokees hunted deer through its thickets.

After a while the scenery began to change. Plantations were closer together. Instead of rude cabins, we had occasional glimpses of palatial residences, surrounded by beautiful groves and parks. And the monotony of the forest was broken by the frequent sight of live oak, palmetto and other Southern trees, till, late in the afternoon, we ran into Savannah.

Savannah has been called a beautiful city. I don't know much about it, but what I saw did not impress me favorably. One thing I do know—I could find better hotel accommodations even in Chicago, than were furnished me by the C. S. Government. We were corralled on some vacant lots, in the southern part of the city—almost out of town.

Some of the boys escaped the guard and went into town, but they were caught and brought back the next day. They then loaded us on the cars—that had been kept ready for us all this time—and crossed the Ogeechee, a river that empties into the Atlantic a short distance south of Savannah.

This river meanders with sluggish current through vast marshes almost anywhere six or eight miles wide, and its broad, flat bottoms make the best rice-producing lands in Georgia. Immense plantations stretch away as far as the eye can reach. Nothing but rice-fields in sight. The planters who own these lands do not live on them. Even the slaves were not kept here except for short intervals while caring for the crop. All have higher and dryer places in which to live.

After crossing the river and its wide marshes, our train stopped in the side track at the first station.

We had the blues. It would not be hard to guard us there. Suppose we slip out and escape our guard, that long trestle-work over which we came will be closely guarded, and we cannot cross that swampy river. Such thoughts filled us with gloom.

We remained at that station all the next day. A great number of trains passed that day, all going south or southwest. (We were on the Savannah & Gulf R. R.) Every train was loaded with household goods, livestock and negroes. The passenger trains were crowded, till every platform was full of men. All seemed excited and uneasy. We begged a daily paper, and found that Sherman was loose in Georgia. Then *we* got excited.

That explained our removal from Camp Lawton. We asked every one that passed, "Where's Sherman?" He was then in the heart of the State, not far from the prison we had left. Every time a train stopped at our station, we would salute its passengers with "John Brown."

The rising generation will never appreciate that song. As sung by the soldiers, it had a power and unction never to be forgotten. It was played and sung in every conquered city of the South. Every prison heard its melody.

We were full of hope. We thought that when Sherman got through to the coast he would send his cavalry and release us. The night before, we were sad and cast down because of the vast swamps that lay between us and home. That night we were full of hope and joy because we thought our forces were coming to our relief.

The next day we were taken farther down the road, and stopped at another station, the name of which I have forgotten; and the day following, we crossed the Altamaha river and stopped at Blackshear station. This station is just north of the Okopinokee swamp, that covers three or four thousand square miles of the southeastern corner of Georgia. The whole country, after crossing the Altamaha is the poorest and dreariest I ever saw.

A series of swamps, ponds and sandy glades in endless monotony. Once in a while we would pass in sight of a habitation, three or four acres partly cleared by deadening the large trees and cutting down the small growth. In the midst of these dead trees, a cabin of one room, with a mud chimney at one end, and a door on one side, no windows—didn't need any, as the cracks were unchinked—is a fair picture of an average home in that part of the State. A corn patch, cultivated among the dead trees, and yielding not more than ten bushels per acre, supplies the family with bread.

A cotton patch clothes it, and the rifle and fishing-rod supply the rest.

If the country looked flat, the citizens looked flatter. They are the class known in the South as the "Poor white trash," against whom even the negro will curl his lip in contempt.

A sample citizen, is tall, lean, flat-chested, dull-eyed, pale-faced, and stoop-shouldered. He has a way of stretching his long, slim neck at almost a right angle with the general perpendicular of his body, which keeps his head a long way in advance. If he should carry an umbrella to protect his head from a rain, the water would run off of it down the back of his neck.

I don't remember seeing a four-wheeled vehicle in that country, except the few army wagons that our guard had with them. We frequently saw two-wheeled carts, sometimes drawn by a yoke of oxen, sometimes by one horse, and in a few instances by one ox. We saw horses harnessed to carts, with a collar of corn-husks and harness composed partly of hickory bark and withes. The driver rides the horse, putting his bare feet on the shafts, which serve as stirrups. This position brings his knees almost on a level with his horse's ears, and gives him quite a picturesque appearance. If he is taking his lady-love out for a ride, she sits flat on the bottom of the cart, while he rides and guides the horse. Romantic—isn't it?

Blackshear is a scrawny town. I believe it is a county-seat, but as I have described the county that sits there, I can let you imagine the seat.

Almost starved and worn out, we landed here, were taken off the cars, and marched into the woods to a new prison.

CHAPTER XVIII.

SENT BACK TO ANDERSONVILLE.

In the pine woods, about a mile from Blackshear, we were corralled on about five acres of ground.

There was no wall or fence to enclose us. A dead-line was staked off, and outside of it another row of stakes marked the line of sentinels, who stood about ten or fifteen steps apart, all around us, ready to shoot any one who passed the first row of stakes.

Had there been nothing between us and liberty except that guard, we could have broken through and escaped; but the memory of those wide rivers and dreary swamps, and the fact that it was now winter, made us hesitate to run a gauntlet of hounds and patrolmen, and probable starvation. Then, too, the fact that they built no wall around us, and no quarters for themselves, made us think they did not intend to keep us there very long.

We drew raw rations, about the same as at Millen prison; but a few of us improved them slightly by "flanking." The trick of "flanking" a ration was not possible at Andersonville or Millen, where we were carefully counted into and out of the pen. But here we were all massed in the grove, and the guard placed around us, and then ordered to form into companies of one hundred to be counted for rations. One rebel sergeant had about ten of these companies to count and report. As soon as one squad had been counted and marked full, the "flanker" would drop out of line, and by careful dodging and skulking would take his place in another hundred, before the sergeant would get to it, and thus get himself counted again. Of course wherever he could succeed in being counted he took a "mess number," and drew a ration. When the rations came in he had to have a chum to assist him, and usually two or three divided the extra ration thus obtained.

When we were counted onto the train to take us away, it was found that the number of men reported for rations exceeded the actual number in the pen about seven hundred. At least we were informed that such was the case by the rebels themselves.

We had been in this place but a few days when we were informed that a special exchange of ten thousand sick and wounded prisoners was ordered to take place immediately, and that two thousand were to be taken from our pen. This news threw us into a fever of excitement; and when, two days later they began to take out the number, the law of self-preservation brought out the worst elements of human nature. Sick men, whose lives depended on their getting out, were cheated out of their chance, and some of the stoutest and heartiest men there feigned sickness and wounds and got away. They were taken to Savannah, where a part of them were exchanged about the middle of December. The remainder were sent back in a few days.

One evening, just at dusk, about a thousand of us broke guard, and took to the woods. We thought to try to find the Atlantic coast, but we were soon caught and brought back. The enterprise failed so completely that it is scarcely worth the mention. I was one of those who tried it. All the comfort we had was the satisfaction of making the Johnnies rattle around lively to overhaul us and get us back.

We stayed at Blackshear about two weeks; I do not remember the exact time. We were then loaded on the cars and taken to Thomasville, which is near the southwest corner of the State. Here we were corralled and guarded in the same manner as at Blackshear,

I think the country around Thomasville is about as fine as can be found in Georgia. The soil is good, and the climate mild enough for figs to grow out of doors.

We were left here about a week, when all who could walk were made to march sixty miles across the country to Albany. I do not know what became of the sick who could not walk. We never saw them any more.

On this march, Tom B——, my old chum of the swamps, slipped his guard and went to a farm-house and got a square meal, and then told what manner of man he was, and let the old citizen arrest him and bring him back.

At Albany we were crowded in and around the depot. Many of the citizens came down to see us and talk with us. The guard was kind, and allowed us to talk with them. Some were pleasant and agreeable, and others were ill-natured and quarrelsome. Some wanted to know what "You-alls want to fight we-uns for." Some asked us to sing a song, and we gave them "John Brown," with a chorus of three or four thousand voices. That song always touched the right spot.

The next day two or three trains of cars backed in. We were soon aboard. Now, where?

To Andersonville!

On Christmas Day. The day of peace and good-will; when all the earth was gladness and song; when all were trying to see how much happiness they could enjoy and give; when there was feasting and merriment, and sweet surprises, in Christian homes! Yes, on that day, as if to make our lives blacker by the contrast of pleasant recollections, we were brought back to Andersonville.

About two o'clock P. M. we were counted through the double gate. Old Wirtz was there, cursing us as we entered. "You come back! You flank me—I keep you,"— blurting out short sentences and long oaths.

About the first of October Tom and I had left that horrible pen, hoping never to see it again. After all our weary toil and changing scenes and prisons, we are back at last to the starting point!

About ten thousand went to Blackshear. Some of them were exchanged; some died; some were left sick at Thomasville,—about seven thousand returned to Andersonville. A few sick ones had remained there all the time, but not many—perhaps two thousand.

We all settled on the south side of the brook. The north side, that had contained a population of twenty thousand in the crowded period of August and September, contained but a few stragglers on the 1st of January. On the south side we were thickly settled, but not crowded as we were before.

CHAPTER XIX.

ANDERSONVILLE IN WINTER.

It was now the dead of winter. It rained about four days of a week, and was cloudy and damp nearly all the time. Heavy east winds prevailed. We seldom saw the sun shine. Our sack-tent, that never did keep the rain out, was now rotten and torn till we had to patch it nearly all over with such scraps of old shirts, pants, or blankets, as we could find.

The rebel authorities allowed a detail of three men from each hundred to go out—under guard—to the woods to pick limbs and such other pieces of wood as we could find, for fuel. There was an abundance of good wood all around us, but we had no axes with which to prepare it, and had to content ourselves with such scraps as old Time and Storm had prepared. The best of it was where pine logs had rotted and left the knots. These, being full of tar, burned freely in the dampest weather.

In this way about two hundred men went out every day, and returned with an armfull or a shoulder-load of wood. We soon picked up all that we could get, near the stockade, and had to go farther and farther into the woods. I think most of our wood was carried three-fourths of a mile. We were too weak to carry a large load so far, but we did our best. I know that when I got out I carried in a load that gave me the thumps.

When we got our wood home, with a railroad spike for a wedge, and a pine knot for a maul, we split it; and broke it up fine so as to make it go as far as possible—and even then we were without wood most of the time,

Think of it! Three men from a hundred go out every day. If you get out to-day, it will be thirty-three days—or nearly five weeks—before your turn comes again! It would take a strong man to carry wood enough to keep him dry and warm for five weeks.

Here, again, the strong took advantage of the week. If a man was sick and weak, some stronger man would give him a chew of tobacco, or a spoonful of rice, for his "turn" to go for wood. Then, with one-fourth his load of wood he could buy two or three times as much rice or tobacco as he paid for the "turn;" and very likely in the course of a week or two, when a cold rain had fallen all night, you would find the weak man, in a hole in the sand, doubled up like a jackknife, chilled to death!

Does some one say, "That must have been a mean set in Andersonville, to treat each other so?" Look around you. Even in the Northern States, I see the strong and shrewd taking advantage of the weak and simple. "Let him that is without sin cast the first stone."

One way we had to keep warm, those damp, chilly days, was to dig a funnel-shaped hole in the sand, about four feet in diameter, and two feet deep. Four of us would sit in this hole. Our feet would be together in the bottom; our knees together in the center; then leaning forward till our heads were almost together, we would spread our blanket over the pile, and draw it down close to the edges—thus keeping in the heat of our bodies and the warmth of our breath. I have sat in such a hole frequently all day, except time enough to draw and eat my rations. Some dug these holes larger and deeper than the one I have described, and eight or ten would get into them.

Those were dreary days. It rained almost constantly during January. There was plenty of timber all around us. We would have gladly cut and carried it, and built huts and fires. There is no apology for not letting us do so. Hundreds chilled to death for want of them. They were *murdered*—brutally, in cold blood!

Once in a while we would have a clear

day, and we would dry our clothes and blankets, take down our tents, and let the sun dry the sand on which we slept, pull off our clothes and kill the vermin on them— and feel comparatively comfortable and happy.

About the first of January a few prisoners were brought in, who told us that Sherman had reached the sea, at Savannah, and had turned northward into Carolina. So the last lingering hope that he would rescue us died within us. A few days later a squad of prisoners came in from the western division of the army, and brought the news of the battle of Nashville, and told us how "Pap" Thomas had utterly crushed Hood's army. Among these prisoners, was one called "Old Beard"—a *nomme de querre*—of my own regiment. He brought us much news from our comrades who escaped when we were captured, and gave us a history of subsequent campaigns, such as only one soldier can give to another.

This was the last reliable news we received till it was all over. I can't describe the suspense, the anxiety, that almost consumed us, and I will not try.

During the winter the guard relaxed much of its sternness and rigor, and many of the men who composed it were willing to enter into conversation and traffic with us, when their officers were not in sight. This gave rise to several manufacturing industries. One was carving pipes. Some of the boys, when they got out for wood, would dig greenbriar-roots, and from these, and other kinds of wood, finely-carved pipes were made. Frequently two or three weeks' labor was expended on a single pipe, which was then sold for a half gallon of "nigger peas," a quart of meal, or three dollars "Confed."

Another branch of business was carving toothpicks. These were made from the bones of meat that we drew, and, like the pipes, they were valuable in proportion to the amount of labor bestowed on them.

Bob Mc—— made toothpicks. His kit of tools consisted of a piece of an old case-knife, one side of it cut full of notches for a saw; a brick-bat, which he used for grindstone, file, and polisher; and a piece of coarse needle fastened into a bone handle, and ground flat-pointed, which served as a drill or boring machine. With such a set of tools, if he had favorable weather, he could turn out two good toothpicks per month.

Still another branch of *business (?)* carried on at this time, was "raising" Confederate notes. Confederate money was poorly made, both in design and execution. The "ones" and "twos," and "tens" and "twenties" were almost alike, except in the figures that told their denomination. If a man could get a one or two-dollar bill, he knew where to take it and have it converted into a ten or twenty—"All work done in the best style of art and warranted to pass." In buying beans or meal with this money, we always aimed to trade so as to get one or two small bills in change so that we could make another "raise." I expect that good brother who thought we stole the sacks from the quartermaster, will think this looks like counterfeiting. It *does* *look* that way, and had those Yanks been caught at it, they might have been sent to Andersonville!—the worst imprisonment I can think of—and sentenced to remain there as long as Confederate money had a value.

CHAPTER XX.

THE GENERAL EXCHANGE.

During the month of February the rebels furnished material, and detailed a lot of prisoners—giving them extra rations—and had three sheds erected.

These sheds were about twenty-five feet wide, by one hundred and fifty long; about five feet high at the eaves, and ten or twelve feet high in the center—roofed with boards, and left open on all sides. They were designed for a shelter for those who had no blankets or tents of any kind; and during a hard rain one thousand men would crowd under each shed. When it was not raining most of the men preferred to remain outside, on account of the vermin—especially fleas—which were so much worse in the dry sand under these roofs than in other parts of the prison.

In the different narratives of Andersonville prison life, I have never seen any account of the building of these sheds; but I am glad to give to the notorious Winder and Wirtz credit for this much humanity. Perhaps the reader thinks it was no great thing to build such sheds.' True. And yet they were a blessing to a number of wretched prisoners who were almost naked, and had there been more of them, and had they been built in the fall, they would have saved many lives.

Thus the winter wore away. March came; and looking over the stockade toward the forest, we could see the burst buds and tender leaves, telling of springtime and a new year. We heard no news from the war, in which we were so intensely interested. What was Grant doing? Where was Sherman? What had become of Thomas since his victory at Nashville? These questions were often asked—but as they were never answered, to ask them only intensified our sadness.

But the great question—the one that took precedence over all others, was: Why don't our Government exchange prisoners and get us out?

It was a hard strain on our patriotism to feel that we were neglected by our own Government. For we believed then, as we learned certainly afterward, that we could have been exchanged had those in charge of our armies so desired.

Many of the men lying on the wet ground by night, and sitting on it by day, had contracted colds, that settled on their lungs. Hundreds had that peculiar cough and that brightness of the cheek and eye, that told us that consumption had set in; and that if they were not soon exchanged they would be beyond the reach of cartel. Many who had despaired of ever getting well, were anxious to go home that they might die among friends.

One day, early in March, an order was

read at the gate, that declared that a general exchange of prisoners had been agreed upon, and that they would begin at once, and empty the prisons in Virginia and Carolina first, and would probably reach Andersonville in two weeks, or ten days.

This news threw the camp into a wild excitement, though I must confess that many of us did not believe it. We had been deceived too often, and this sounded so good that we suspected it was being done to make us docile while they were moving us somewhere else.

But in a few days they gave us copies of papers that contained accounts of the release of prisoners from Richmond and Saulsbury. Then we began to believe and to grow feverish with excitement.

In due time rebel officers came in and began to enroll names, putting down rank and regiment. The first call was to take out all the sick: but they gave us the wink, and told us that if any one had any greenbacks, or gold, they would enroll him as sick, and take him out on the first train.

John C—, Cudge S— and I were partners

in the sack-tent, and had been bunk-mates during the whole of our prison life, except when I ran away.

John had a gold breast-pin that cost two or three dollars before the war, which somehow had escaped all the searchings and had remained in his possession till then. He took it out of its hiding-place, examined and polished it, and said, "Boys, I am going to see what I can do with this; for as likely as not they will not get out more than two or three train-loads till something will happen to break the cartel, and we will be left again."

He went; but soon came back with the news that they had all they could take that day. But they told him there would be another train in a day or two.

So we had to wait a day or two. Then they came again, and John went to buy his liberty with the breast-pin. He came back and said—

"Boys, I tried to take you both out on my breast-pin, but couldn't. I can take one—which shall it be?"

Cudge and I looked at each other, and

both sprang to our feet. As soon as we could speak without choking, we both told him we would leave it to him. We all three sat down and began to talk of home—how long it would take to go; how glad we would be to get there; how glad others would be to see us returned at last, alive! Oh, those dear ones! Could it be possible that we would see them once more! We talked rapidly—excitedly—almost wildly; but every little while Cudge and I would look at each other and choke down. We knew that one must remain behind, for only one could go. I went away for a short time, and when I returned John looked at me and said,

"I reckon I will take Cudge."

"So you leave me to die and rot by myself!"

They both tried to cheer me, by telling me that I would soon follow them; but I wouldn't be cheered—I knew something would happen; the exchange would be stopped, and I would languish and die. I felt very much as I did when I was recaptured after my run-away.

With a heart full of gloomy forebodings and bitterness, I went with them to the gate. I made Cudge promise to write a letter to my folks at home, telling them that I was alive at that date. I told him to fix it up as good as he could, so as not to cause mother more sorrow than was actually necessary.

The whole prison was crowded around the gate; and as the names were called by a loud-voiced rebel, some countenance would light up with joy as he answered, "Here!" and you would see him struggle through the crowd to the gate and disappear through the wicket.

We three stood together, near the dead-line. "John Carey!" called the reb. *Here!*—and he was through the wicket before I could look at him. "Allen Spencer!" *Here!* Cudge gave me his hand: "Good-bye, Oats." "Good-bye, Cudge,"—and he slipped through the wicket and the door swung to.

I staggered back through the crowd. They were gone! I had no farther interest in the gate or in the crowd. I was alone! My comrades had left me to die! Blinded by my tears, and sick through the intensity of my feelings, I reached our tent—*my* tent, now—and lay down.

Our talk of home had given me the blues. I could see nothing but darkness and sorrow, misery and death! I was unreasonable—mad at everything and everybody, because I could not get out. Like Job's wife, I was ready to "curse God and die."

But I got over it in a day or two. How do we get down and up under the trials and disappointments of life? Who can tell?

The prisoners were taken to Vicksburg, Mississippi, for exchange. There was one train-load taken after the one that took my comrades. Then came word that Wilson's Cavalry (U. S.) had raided through Mississippi and Alabama, and destroyed the railroad over which they were shipping the prisoners, so the exchange was stopped.

About eight thousand came from Blackshear—and about four thousand remained when Wilon's raid stopped the exchange.

CHAPTER XXI.

OUR LAST PRISON.

For two weeks after the exchange was stopped, our excitement was kept at white heat by rumors of Wilson's raid. At first, he was in Mississippi; next we heard rumors of his movements in Alabama. He was coming toward us, and we began to feel confident that instead of being exchanged we would be released. This filled us with hope and put us in fine spirits. The whole camp seemed cheerful, and confident that we would soon get out, in some way.

After my chums left me I went into partnership with Bob Mc—, a man who belonged to the same company that I did. He was captured at Chicamauga, in September, 1863; was taken to Richmond, spent the winter on Belle Isle; was taken from there to Danville, Va., and thence to Andersonville. He stood seventeen months of prison life—they couldn't kill him! He was a short, thick-set man, thirty-eight or forty years of age. He was quite bald-headed; and had had the scurvy for almost a year. During the crowded term of 1864, he was taken to the tent hospital, outside the stockade. He was almost dead then, but he ate sumac-berries freely, and got better; so much better, that he and a comrade started one night to run away.

It was a poor run. They became entangled in the swamps, and only got five or six miles. The next day they were missed. The Andersonville pack of hounds were turned loose, and they were treed before night. For this grave sin of trying to get away, Bob was put in the stocks! They had a number of these implements of torture in front of Wirtz's quarters. The peculiar style of the set in which Bob was fastened, was a strong frame, with four posts securing the ends of two heavy timbers, like joists; in each of these was a semi-circular notch. The joists were brought together horizontally so as to fit the notches around a man's neck, and fastened there by keys at the ends. They were then lowered so as to depress the body about three inches lower than its natural position—so that the victim could neither straighten up nor sit down.

The next morning after Bob's recapture, his neck was fastened in this machine, and he stood in this painful position *twelve hours*. It was a hot day in September, and the sun poured his burning rays upon Bob's bare bald head all day.

They did not give him a bite to eat nor a drop to drink during the twelve hours, although he begged piteously for water. About two o'clock, the sun baking his head caused him to become unconscious for an instant, and his legs gave way; the back of his head and his chin struck the timbers with a crack that brought him to consciousness suddenly, and made him think for a moment that his neck was broken. Though his poor, scurvied limbs ached as if they would break, he stood it until sunset. He was then released, received a ration of bread, and was turned into the stockade.

Bob was a jolly, good-natured fellow to be with; and by the partnership, we had a pretty fair equipment—for Andersonville. I had my tent, my half blanket, my pan, that I made out of the car-roofing, and a railroad-spike. Bob had a tent as good as mine, which we spread over mine, and as the holes hardly ever came in both at the same place one patched the other bravely. He had a wooden bucket which he had made, that would hold a quart; an old sock, which we used for a meal-sack when we drew our rations; it was one of those old regulation woolen socks, but it proved to be a very useful article in our household economy. Then he had his toothpick tools, and we became partners in that industry.

About four o'clock one day, toward the last of March, two long trains stopped at the station. A guard was detailed in a hurry. The counting-sergeants came in and ordered us to get ready to go out at once.

"How many are you going to take?"

"Every —— —- —— has to be out a-foah mawnin'!"

We guessed at once that Wilson was coming our way, so we asked—

"Where's Wilson's raiders?"

He answered in one long word that sounded like, "Damifino!"—which we interpreted to mean that he didn't wish to tell.

We passed the word around our part of the prison, "Let's take the last train, and may be Wilson will catch us." They hurried us all they could. The first train was loaded, and pulled out about sunset. Ours did not get loaded till after dark. They would count off eighty men, and crowd them up to a car door, and keep saying—"Hurry up, dah! hurry up, dah!"

Our old chum, Tom, with whom the reader is well acquainted, was in the midst of such a squad, and instead of climbing into the car he crept under it, and passing under the depot building, *got left.* He kept himself hid till Wilson came, and so he got away and found his regiment.

In our train were five flat-cars, containing about three hundred prisoners. I was on one of these. They were well to the rear of the train, with perhaps two or three box-cars and a caboose behind. The guard did not seem to fancy these flats, so most of them climbed onto the box-cars ahead of us. Soon after we started, some one discovered that there were but three guards on the five flats, and conceived the bold project of cutting the train and giving them the grand bounce. The plan was, to uncouple the rear boxes, and as soon as they were sufficiently to the rear—a mile or so— to then uncouple the flats; and as soon as they stopped, to jump off and take to the woods. We knew that those three guards could not stop us, even if they tried.

Going down a grade, the pin was drawn; and we soon saw the space widen, and the rear cars grew dim in the distance. Now for another little grade, and then—

But our guard was too vigilant. One of

those on the flats discovered that the rear was gone, and by running over us and jumping from car to car, he managed to alarm the guard on the boxes ahead of us, and soon had two men guarding each coupling. But the train ran about four miles before they made the engineer understand that he had lost a part of his train. He then ran on to the first station, and left us while he went back for the rear.

The Johnnies were badly scared, and terribly indignant at this delay. The officer in command flourished his pistol around us, and swore that if he knew who uncoupled the train he would shoot him! But he did not know. It filled us with exultation and happiness to see the rebs so uneasy.

About daylight we ran into Macon, and stopped, but they did not take us off the cars. From our train we could see up into the business part of town, and noticed a number of large, white flags floating over the principal houses. We asked a negro what they were for, and he said—

"Specks de Yanks is comin'!"

The officers in charge of us held a hurried

consultation with the authorities. The engine was turned around and hitched to the other end of our train, and by eight o'clock we were steaming away down the same road we came up the night before. What did they mean—taking us back to Andersonville?

About two or three o'clock P. M. we passed Andersonville, and from the cars we took our last look at that pen of woe. They took us to Albany—to Thomasville, over the same route that we came in December. "Where are we going?" The rebs told us that they were taking us around that way to Savannah, to exchange us—but, as usual, they lied.

They took us eastward from Thomasville to a junction, the name of which I have forgotten. There we took another road, and ran southward till we struck the Jacksonville & Tallehasse railroad, thence eastward again till we reached Lake City, Florida.

In sight of the railroad, about four miles east of Lake City, on an island—or more properly, a peninsula—in a vast cypress swamp, we were corralled for the last time. Our prison was a palmetto-covered knoll, of about two acres area, surrounded on all sides by swamp and water, except a narrow low neck across which a corduroy road connected us with the main land.

Here we had plenty of fuel. Pine and cypress logs lay in rich abundance all about us. When we were there, during April, the weather was warm and dry. The trees were full of foliage, and all looked like summer-time. The weather was so pleasant that we hardly needed clothing.

I had gone without a shirt all winter, using my blouse instead. It had now become so rotten and ragged that it was not worth picking the lice off for all the protection it afforded, so I threw it away. My wardrobe then consisted of pants, ending in a neat (?) fringe about the knee, and a leathern gun-sling, which did duty as a suspender. From the waist, upward, I was smoked and tanned to the complexion of well-cured bacon.

Do not think that I was not as well-dressed as was fashionable, for the *poor* did not enjoy a gun-sling to hold their pants up. Bob had a pair of pants, and a shirt, minus the sleeves, that he had made out of a blouse and piece of sack; he also had a piece of pants-leg, which he used for a hat. He would pull one end of it on his head, and throwing the other end backward, he looked like a Grand Turk in full dress.

While we were in this prison our rations consisted of a pint of meal per day. We were there one month, and drew nothing but meal during our stay—we did not even draw salt to season it. Bob and I made ours into mush most of the time. There was plenty of it, such as it was. One day one of the guards shot an alligator, about eight feet long, which he gave to the prisoners. Some of the boys tried steaks off of its tail. That was the only meat eaten in that prison.

CHAPTER XXII.

"THE STAR-SPANGLED BANNER."

It was the last of April, 1865. Thirty-three hundred prisoners were encamped on that little island. The quartermaster brought in our rations, and we noticed more sacks than usual. What does it mean? The old quartermaster gave a knowing wink, and said he was going to fatten us. We wisely guessed that they were going to move us.

The rations measured out three pints of meal per man. Bob and I had our sock full, shook down, and packed—and then had to take part of our rations in his bucket.

Next morning we were up by times, and were soon all ready and waiting to see what would happen. Soon a train of cars came down. We were loaded on, and went eastward a few miles—as far as the rails were laid, as the iron had been taken off this road, to mend others, nearly all the way from Jacksonville to Lake City.

When we got to the end of the railroad we were ordered off the cars, and marched out on the old road bed ahead of the engine. The colonel who had command of our guard then made us a speech.

He told us that they were tired of guarding us. They knew our time was out, and that we were anxious to get home. They were going to the front to fight, and so had decided to turn us loose. He advised us to go home, and stay there; and to tell our friends at the North that we "could never whip the rebels in the world!" He told us to follow the railroad-bed and it would take us to Jacksonville—which was in possession of the Yanks.

This is the substance of his speech, although he embellished it with much boasting and many oaths.

The whole speech was a lie. He was included in Johnson's surrrender to Sherman, and was then under orders to go to Tallehasse to turn over his arms to the United States authorities. This we learned after we got out.

After this speech the guard opened ranks, and we marched out. "Good-bye, Johnnies!" "Good-bye, Yanks!"—were the parting salutations.

Were we really free? Could we go or stop, as we pleased? It was like a dream! It was so sudden—so unexpected. Our minds were not prepared for it. We could hardly realize it. We felt like shouting! A great load had been suddenly lifted—but how? What had become of it?

I do not remember how far we had to travel. It seems like it was forty-two miles from our camp to Jacksonville; but I can't remember how far they took us on the cars. I think it was eight or ten miles, but am not sure.

In our excitement at being turned loose

we started off at too rapid a rate. Soon the sick ones began to fall by the way. Some went a mile and gave out; some two or three, and failed; others five or six—and so we were strung out all along the road. Bob and I kept well up with the head of the column. Bob was lame with scurvy in his limbs, but he was plucky; and I, being in fair health, carried his baggage.

We went as far as we could that day, and hid in the palmettos at night. We were actually afraid the rebels would change their minds, and come on and overtake us; hence we hid carefully.

The next morning we were up bright and early. A goodly number of us were on the road, trudging eastward, by sun-up. About noon we came to a creek, whose waters bore the dark tea-color of the swamp. As it flowed smoothly over a sandy bed, and we were tired, we stopped and bathed, and were much refreshed.

About the middle of the afternoon we saw an object that looked like a man on horseback, a mile or so down the road. When we came nearer it was gone. We came to the place and there, sure enough, was the sign of a picket-post. But what had become of him? We did not go far till we saw a troop of cavalry coming toward us. They were too far for us to distinguish their uniform, so we halted. Stragglers kept closing up till we had quite a company, uncertain what to do.

The cavalry halted, and drew up in line. Then two men were sent toward us to see what we were. They doubtless judged by our unmilitary appearance that we were not very formidable. When the two soldiers came near enough for us to see their uniform, a wild shout rent the air. It was taken up by stragglers in the rear, and carried to others still farther back—to be repeated again and again,—giving new vigor to weary limbs that had almost refused to do duty longer. That shout doubtless reached three or four miles back along that road.

Yes, sir! It *was* the United States uniform!

I have seen a good many fine clothes in my life—but I never saw anything, before or since, that looked so pretty as those cavalry jackets!

We started toward them at once, and went to where the troop was waiting. If we were glad to see their clothes, they were *mad* when they saw ours.

When the commander of that troop found out who we were, and looked at our rags and our wretchedness, he stood up in his stirrups and swore a terrible oath of vengeance. And scarcely one of those bearded, swarthy troopers but turned away his face to hide the tears that would come up, as he looked in amazement at our haggard countenances, meager skeletons and filthy rags.

The captain told us that it was but three miles to Jacksonville, and that he would go and have tents and rations ready for us.

We came to the infantry picket-line, and there dropped down for a few minutes' rest. There were probably three hundred of us together, forming the head of our column. While we were resting we asked the officer of the guard for news, and he told us that Richmond had fallen,—that Lee had surrendered,—that Johnson had surrendered to Sherman,—that the Confederacy had gone to staves, and that *Lincoln was dead!*

It is no use trying to describe the effect of this news on men in our condition. My readers would not understand it—language is too feeble.

We did not need rest after we heard the news. We were not a bit tired. We arose and started toward the town, which was yet three-fourths of a mile distant.

About half way to town we met a "field band" and "colors." We were wild enough before, but when we met the flag we went stark, raving crazy. If we had all been drunk on laughing gas, we would not have acted worse. Old scurvied fellows who could not straighten a limb danced around like puppets and kicked the sand twenty feet high. Some cried—some laughed—some danced—some sung—some prayed—some swore. It was a wonderful medley. We had divers gifts, but the same spirit.

One tall, ragged skeleton began trying to sing—

"Wrap the flag around me, boys,"

and, reaching out his gaunt, fleshless arms, he caught the folds of the flag, and began to wind it about his vermin-eaten shoulders. Another, and another, joined in the song, and caught at the flag, till soon they had it trailing on the ground, with from twenty to fifty boys sprawling under and over it.

The band stopped playing, and gazed in amazement at the treatment their flag was receiving. Those not engaged in the flag-scuffle, noticing that the music had stopped, gathered handfulls of sand, and, throwing it on the band, told them to give us "The Star-Spangled Banner" or we would bury them right there.

The band commenced to play the music, and the boys to sing the words. They got on somehow until they reached—

"O, say, does the star-spangled banner yet wave?"

when, raising one wild whoop, they rushed to the band, upsetting one another in the sand, silencing the music, scattering the drummers, and yelling—"This is God's country!"

Yes, I remember it all; but, reader, you will not see it in my tame description. If I could paint for you the untrimmed, tangled hair, that hung in matted tags or stood out in all directions above brows that had once been noble and fair, but were now all blotched and stained by disease; if I could paint the hollow cheek, the dull eyes, the fleshless limbs, hands like birds' claws—the filthy, vermin-eaten rags; and could then put my picture through all the contortions of unrestrained motion,—even then, you could not see all that is in my memory.

As soon as sense returned, we were told to turn to the left and cross a little creek, beyond which we would camp. We came to the creek, found a box of soap on the bank, and with the shout—"This is God's country, for here's soap!"—more than a hundred men, each with a bar in his hand, plunged into the stream and tried to turn it into soapsuds.

CHAPTER. XXIII.

HOMEWARD BOUND

The place selected for our camp was a side-hill pasture, with a few trees scattered over it for shade. The military authorities had made the best preparation they could, in the brief time since the captain of cavalry had reported us.

A load of hospital tents had been hauled out and distributed for our use, but we did not put them up that night. We did not need them. Bob and I carried one up under a tree and folded it to lie on.

It was about sun-set when we reached our

camping-ground. Stragglers kept coming in till ten o'clock, when, of the thirty-three hundred that had been turned loose, about seven hundred had reached our lines.

Just before dark a wagon came loaded with bread—the first wheat bread we had seen in a long time. We got a loaf apiece and ate it. Then came four barrels of boiled meat—the kind known to the trade as "mess pork," but known to the soldiers by a different name. We secured a good piece of that, and ate it. Then came coffee by the barrel. We took our old bucket and drew a quart of that, and drank it.

Then Bob said he wouldn't go down the hill again, no matter what they brought. Presently the cry was raised, "They are issuing whiskey." I proposed to Bob that we go and get our share, but he said he was too tired. I then told him I would go and draw his ration, and bring it to him. I went, told the man I had a "pard" who was sick, and drew both rations in our bucket, and went back. When I got to our tree, Bob was gone, so I set the whiskey down to wait till he came. Soon he came limping up the hill. After I had gone, he became anxious, for fear they would not give me his ration, so he limped down, took his turn, and had drawn and drank his 'gill.' We made equitable division of what was in the cup, and thus had three gills to two men.

We had travelled about twenty miles that day, and ought to have been tired, but the excitement, the pork, the coffee and the whiskey, took away all drowsiness. We sat and talked of home, and what we would do when we got there, till far into the night. Finally we decided that we must sleep, or we would not be fit for anything next day. So we lay down and remained silent a good while, but I never was wider awake in my life. Bob lay so still that I could not tell whether he was asleep or not, so I whispered softly, "Bob!"

"What do you want?"

"I can't sleep."

"Neither can I."

After awhile we decided that we *must* go to sleep.

We lay quite still for a long time. Suddenly Bob arose to a sitting posture, and gathering our sock, which still contained about a pint of meal, he called out, *"Oats! Here goes the last of the Confederacy,"* and taking the sock by the toe, he began to swing it around his head, strewing the meal all over me, himself, and our tent. That put sleep out of the question, so we got up and chatted, till we heard the bugle across the creek, blow reveille.

When it was day, we found that eleven of those who had struggled so bravely to keep up, and had greeted the flag with the head of the column, were DEAD.

That mother and sister, waiting in their darkened northern home, may never know how hard their dear one tried to come, nor how he almost succeeded.

A train of wagons and ambulances, with surgeons and nurses, went out on our back track, to look after those who had given out by the way.

It took them three days to go and return. They found a good many who, with a little help, were able to struggle into camp; some who were past walking, some dying—

and some already dead. They were scattered along the entire road, to where we were turned out. The dead were buried, and the living brought in and cared for.

We stayed in Jacksonville about three weeks. During this time we drew new clothes, had our hair trimmed, beards shaved, and changed till we hardly knew each other. We were then put on a steam boat and taken to Fernandina, where we were put on an ocean steamer, called "Cassandra."

That evening we steamed out upon the Atlantic, and began to enjoy (?) a sea voyage. We put in at Port Royal, and took aboard a large lot of ice, and four or five *nice* military officers. We asked those who loaded the ice, what it was for, and they told us it was furnished by the Sanitary Commission, for the sick soldiers. We supposed that meant us—but we soon found we were mistaken. It was kept in a refrigerator built on purpose, that opened on the top deck, and was securely locked up. They expected it to be kept for the use of the ship's officers and those nice military fellows in the cabin. *We* thought it a clear case of misappropriation. The next morning when the steward went to get a piece, to fix up mint-slings, and such luxuries, he found the door wide open and the ice all gone.

You guess!

In three or four days we reached Fortress Monroe. Then Annapolis, where we disembarked. Then over the Baltimore & Ohio railroad to Camp Chase, Ohio—where we were discharged on the 16th of June. Then home.

I was to my folks as one from the dead. They had given me up. Mother told me that she would never be any surer that I was dead, unless I should die at home, than she had been. What a time we had. There were no dry eyes.

Does the reader ask what became of my old comrades, Cudge and John? They were *murdered* by an agent of the United States Government. They got to Vicksburg, and were exchanged all right, and were to be sent North for discharge.

The steamboat "Sultana" was at the

landing. If she had been in good condition, five or six hundred men would have been a good load for her; but the inspectors had condemned her as *unsafe*. Yet in the face of this fact, the agent was induced by some means to give her the extraordinary load of *eighteen hundred human beings!* She did not run far, till she exploded and burned up. Nearly all on board perished.

Charley Higgins, of my company, one of the few survivors of that catastrophe, told me this: John, Cudge, and himself had lain down between the engines; Charley in the rear, John in the middle, and Cudge in front, or next to the boilers. When the boilers burst, Charley and John sprang up; but seeing Cudge lie still, Charley ran to him and took hold of him to help him up. But something had struck and killed him! John and Charley then ran and jumped into the river among the hundreds of struggling mortals. Charley was picked up about five miles below, swimming and floating with the current. John was never found.

SPEECH OF GEN. GARFIELD
AT THE ANDERSONVILLE REUNION, AT TOLEDO, OHIO, OCTOBER 3, 1879.

"MY COMRADES, LADIES AND GENTLEMEN: I have addressed a great many audiences. but I never before stood in the presence of one that I felt so wholly unworthy to speak to. A man who came through the war without being shot or made a prisoner, is almost out of place in such an assemblage as this. While I have listened to you this evening I have remembered the words of a distinguished English gentleman, who once said that 'he was willing to die for his country, but he would not do a mean act to save both his king and his country.' Now, to say that a man is willing to die for his country, is a good deal; but these men who sit before us have said a great deal more than that. I would like to know where the man is that would calmly step out on the platform and say, 'I am ready to starve to death for my country!' That is an enormous thing to say; but there is a harder thing than that. Find a man, if you can, who will walk out before this audience and say, 'I am willing to become an idiot for my country!' How many men could you find who would volunteer to become idiots for life for their country? Now, let me make this statement to you, fellow-citizens: One hundred and eighty-eight thousand such men as this were captured by the rebels who were fighting our Government.

"One hundred and eighty-eight thousand! How many is that? They tell me there are four thousand five hundred men and women in this building to-night. Multiply this mighty audience by forty and you will have about one hundred and eighty-eight thousand. Forty times this great audience were prisoners of war to the enemies of our country. And to every man of that enormous company there stood open night and day the offer—'If you will join the Rebel army, and lift up your hand against your flag, you are free!'"

A voice—"That's so!"

Gen. Garfield—"'And you shall have food, and you shall have clothing, and you shall see wife, and mother, and child.'"

A voice—"We didn't do it, though."

Gen. Garfield—"And do you know that out of that one hundred and eighty-eight thousand there were less than three thousand who accepted the offer? And of those three thousand, perhaps nine-tenths of them did it with the mental reservation that they would desert at the earliest hour—the first moment there was an opportunity."

A voice—"That's so."

Gen. Garfield—"But one hundred and eighty-five thousand out of the one hundred and eighty-eight thousand said, 'No! not to see wife again; not to see child again; not to avoid starvation; not to avoid idiocy; not to avoid the most loathsome of loathsome deaths, will I lift this hand of mine against my country, forever!' Now, we praise the ladies for their patriotism; we praise our good citizens at home for their patriotism; we praise the gallant soldiers who fought and fell. But what were all these things compared with that yonder? I bow in reverence. I would stand with unsandaled feet in the presence of such heroism and such suffering; and I would say to you, fellow-citizens, such an assemblage as this has **never yet before** met on this great earth!

"Who have reunions? I will not trench upon forbidden ground, but let me say this: Nothing on the earth and under the sky can call men together for reunions except ideas that have immortal truth and immortal life in them. The animals fight. Lions and tigers fight as ferociously as did you. Wild beasts tear to the death, but they never have reunions. Why? Because wild beasts do not fight for ideas. They merely fight for blood. All these men and all their comrades went out inspired by two immortal ideas: first, that liberty shall be universal in America; and second, that this old flag is the flag of a Nation, and not of a State—that the Nation is supreme over all people and all corporations. Call it a State; call it a section; call it a South; call it a North; call it anything you wish, and yet, armed with the nationality that God gave us, this is a Nation against all State-sovereignty and secession whatever! It is the immortality of that truth that makes these reunions, and that makes this one. You believed it on the battle-field, you believed it in the hell of Andersonville, and you believe it to-day, thank God! **and you will believe it to the last gasp.**"

Voices—"Yes, we will!" "That's so!" etc.

Gen. Garfield—"Well, now, fellow-citizens and fellow-soldiers—but I am not worthy to be your fellow in this work—I thank you for having asked me to speak to you."

Cries of—"Go on! Go on!" "Talk to us some more!"—etc.

"I want to say simply that I have had one opportunity only to do you any service. I did hear a man who stood by my side in the halls of legislation—the man that offered on the floor of Congress the resolution that any man who commanded colored troops should be treated as a pirate, and not as a soldier—I heard that man calmly say, with his head up in the light, in the presence of this American people, that the Union soldiers were as well treated and as kindly treated in all the Southern prisons as were the rebel soldiers in all the Northern prisons."

Voices—"Liar!" "Liar!" "He was a liar!" [Groans, hisses, and a storm of indignation.]

Gen. Garfield—"I heard him declare that no kinder men ever lived than Gen. Winder and his Commander-in-chief, Jeff Davis. And I took it upon myself to overwhelm him with the proof that the tortures you suffered, the wrongs done to you, were suffered and done with the knowledge of the Confederate authorities, from Jeff Davis down—that it was a part of their policy to make you idiots and skeletons, and to exchange your broken and shattered bodies and dethroned minds for strong, robust, well-fed rebel prisoners. That policy, I affirm, has never had its parallel for atrocity in the civilized world."

A voice—"That's so!"

Gen. Garfield—"It was never heard of in any land since the dark ages closed upon the earth. While history lives, men have memories. We can forgive and forget all other things before we can forgive and forget this.

"Finally, and in conclusion, I am willing, and I think that I speak for thousands of others—I am willing to see all the bitterness of the late war buried in the grave of our dead. I would be willing that we should imitate the condescending, loving kindness of Him who planted the green grass on the battle-fields and let the fresh flowers bloom on all the graves alike. I would clasp hands with those who fought against us, make them my brethren and forgive all the past, only on one supreme condition: that it be admitted in practice, acknowledged in theory, that the cause for which we fought and you suffered, was and is and forever more will be right, eternally right. That the cause for which they fought was and forever will be the cause of treason and wrong. Until that is acknowledged, my hand shall never grasp any rebel's hand across any chasm, however small."

A VISIT TO ANDERSONVILLE.

A correspondent of the Boston *Herald* who recently visited the site of the prison at Andersonville, writes as follows:

"Anderson is the name of a station on the Southwestern Railroad, about sixty miles, or two hours' ride, from Macon. It is nothing but a railroad station, and the only other thing besides the railroad which characterizes the spot, is the immense Union Cemetery, of some twenty acres, over which floats the Star-Spangled Banner. The Cemetery is located on the spot where the prisoners were buried, and the trenches were dug with such precision and regularity that the soldiers were not generally disturbed, but allowed to remain as their comrades interred them, working under the watchful eyes and fixed bayonets of the

Georgia Home-Guard. The Cemetery is surrounded by a stout brick wall, with an iron gate, and is under the supervision of a Superintendent, who lives on the grounds. It is a plain spot. There is not much attempt made to ornament this city of our martyred dead. It would take a great deal of even such influences as plants and flowers possess to dispel the melancholy memories that haunt this hill in the pine woods of South Georgia.

"Southerners shun the spot, but the Cemetery is much visited by Northern travelers, and the register in the Superintendent's lodge contains many strange inscriptions besides the names of the visitors. One lady asks the forgiveness of God for the murderers of her brother, who sleeps in the Cemetery. Sentiments of passionate denunciation are more frequent. Occasionally a man who was in the stockade turns up among the visitors. These men, whatever their natural temper, the Superintendent says, can almost be distinguished by the effects of fear, dread, and vivid recollection, which come back like a shock into their faces as they again stand on the now quiet and sunlit scene of their war experiences.

"In the Cemetery the ground is of a general level, and the graves of the known and unknown, properly separated, range in rows, closely laid, as far as the eye can reach. There are actually buried on this elevation *thirteen thousand, seven hundred and fifteen men!* The soldier whose identity was preserved by his comrades is marked in his resting-place by a white marble stone, rising eighteen inches above the level of the ground. A square marble block with the word 'Unknown,' is repeated about one thousand times in the Cemetery. There was no necessity for the contractor to swell his bill with mule-bones in filling up this burial-place. There were bones, and millions of bones; bones ready at hand when he began his work to occupy him till long after he was wearied of it and longed to see it done. The bodies of fourteen thousand men, who perished not where death was neck and neck with life—on the battle-field —but in the comparative (?) security of prison walls.

"Part of the stockade is still standing. There were two rows of trees, one inside the other. The outer row has fallen down, save for a few posts here and there, but a large part of the inner wall still stands. Trees have grown up around the old pen, and a thick growth of underbrush now covers the site of the prison. No traces of the famous brook that ran through the stockade remain, nor the wonderful wells dug by the prisoners. It is all now a mild and peaceful section of the country. Many of the soldiers in the Cemetery have handsome headstones erected to their memories by friends in the North, and efforts are frequently made to have certain graves 'kept green' with flowers and a shower-pot."

www.ingramcontent.com/pod-product-compliance
Lightning Source LLC
Chambersburg PA
CBHW020910230426
43666CB00008B/1388